YOU ARE

THE

CHOSEN ONE

MASTERING YOUR ASCENT:
A TRANSFORMATIVE GUIDE TO UNLOCK YOUR TRUE POTENTIAL

M D Jenkins

Instagram: @MJsChallenge
TikTok: @MJsChallenge

ISBN: 9798332848766

Date of Publication: 18 July 2024

This book is a work of nonfiction. Names, characters,
businesses, organisations,
places, events, and incidents either are the products
of the author's
imagination or are used fictitiously. Any resemblance
to actual persons, living
or dead, events, or locales is entirely coincidental.

Printed in United Kingdom

Dear Special Reader,

Writing this book has been fully a pure labour of love and an act of sharing the lessons I have learned on my own journey of self-discovery and growth. My hope and aim is that, through these pages, you find inspiration, guidance, and the courage to welcome your **unique** path.

As someone who has wrestled with the challenges of a fixed mindset, I understand the transformative power that comes from adopting a growth mindset. It's my belief that, by recognising our ability to learn, adapt, and overcome, we can unlock our true potential and lead lives filled with purpose, joy, and fulfilment.

This book is not just a culmination of my personal experiences, but also the result of countless hours of research, introspection, and the wisdom of those who have come before me and around me in the wider world.

It's my sincere desire that the words contained within will resonate with you and will continue to inspire and guide you as you navigate through life.

Remember, you are the chosen one. You have the power to shape your destiny and create a life that aligns with your deepest values and aspirations.

Contents

"Formal education will make you a living; self-education will make you a fortune"

NEED TO TALK ABOUT!

Jim Rohn

INTRODUCTION

Have you ever felt discouraged from pursuing your dreams? Maybe you faced rejection, criticism, or even mistreatment that made you feel like you didn't have what it takes to succeed. It's a frustrating feeling, knowing deep down that you have a passion, a purpose, a dream, but feeling like the odds are stacked against you.

Why do we allow ourselves to stop dreaming? Why would we give up on something that fuels us, that gives us hope and excitement for the future? Maybe it's fear of failure, fear of disappointment, or fear of what others may think. But what if you could learn how to overcome those fears, to silence the doubts and naysayers, to reignite that spark of hope within you? In this book, I will share my own journey of overcoming the odds and the self-doubt against me in order for me to pursue my dreams, and guide you through the steps I took, to do the same. It's time to start dreaming again, and creating the life you know you deserve.

As a young boy growing up, I had a big dream of being an actor. Whatever stage I was on, I wanted to shine. I wanted to live in America and live the American Dream. You know what I mean, the dream where you can have it all.

Throughout my childhood, America called out to me, day-dreaming of having a big house in the Beverly Hills suburbs with a pool out the back on an acre of land, being liked and respected in my professional industry and getting an expensive Mercedes Benz like one at those sweet 16 parties on MTV. If you haven't guessed it yet, I am a millennial.

I was the kid who never really cared about what others thought and never even bothered guessing what they were thinking. I was the sort of child who liked what they liked; did what felt right in their heart; had no inhibitions; stood up in front of any crowd, giving speeches, singing, dancing or acting. It was always a performance. I always wanted to be the lead in every school play and I knew both my lines and everybody else's too.

I could memorise entire scripts and act with everything I had inside me, visualising the character and going for it. Putting on a show was my favourite thing to do and they may not all have said it, but everyone who watched me had a really good time. I could feel their energy. My feelings, back then told me I was destined to be an actor and I was determined in my head to make it big. I was cocksure I could make people feel something through my performances and that's what kept me wanting to continue. I was driven at this point in my life to make that dream come true.

This all changed when I went to high school. I walked in with a vision in my head, picturing having a locker that I could put all my books in and have my own personality displayed in the inside drawer like they did in all the 90s teen movies. I would become insanely popular because of my outgoing, fun and confident personality and it would be a smooth ride for the next few years to college. To say I was wrong is the biggest understatement! Despite my high expectations, I quickly realised I was an outsider in what felt like a sea of popular kids. I felt out of place and overwhelmed by all the changes I encountered in the new environment.

When people say high school was challenging for them, boy, I genuinely believe them. I walked in with a smile on my face, telling everyone I wanted to be an actor and live in America, becoming a famous international star. Only a few days in, someone turned around to me and said:

"Do you think someone like **you** could ever be a movie star?"

I replied confident but confused "Yes, why? What do you mean someone like me?"

"Well, losers like you get nowhere in life, **you'll never be chosen**"

I was shocked and honestly couldn't get it out of my head. Am I really a loser? It was the strangest feeling because inside, I felt like a winner. It was the first time anyone had taken control and had power over my thoughts before. It was so scary to me. I felt winded and couldn't think clearly. I tried to think positively, that would normally turn away any negative thoughts, but it felt like an uphill battle from that point on.

My thoughts were continuing to race because I had been begging my mum to take the following Saturday off work so I could audition for the upcoming Harry Potter movie that day. They had open auditions and I really wanted to be a part of the experience.

In my mind, I was determined to do it, it was my dream. Mum took the day off work, drove me there and then something strange rushed over me and I refused to go in, I became terrified, I shouted and cried and felt so trapped. My thoughts were flying around my head, I could not get the thought of me being a loser, not getting chosen out of my head, I froze up. I didn't realise it at the time but this was the start of my journey with anxiety.

My mum comforted me, hugged me tight and told me that it was okay but that I should never be scared to pursue my dreams. We drove away and I was so disappointed in myself, wondering where all my confidence had gone?!

It was truly the first time I felt overwhelming anxiety when it came to pursuing what I wanted to do. It wasn't nervousness, it was pure doubt. It even makes me emotional over 20 years later because I know they would have loved me as I was back then. Even if they didn't love me, I would have enjoyed myself, the feeling of just being there and doing it.

As I write this now, the memory of caring so deeply about a single comment from someone who knew nothing about me baffles me. However, that one remark managed to derail my progress towards my dreams, leaving me feeling inadequate and lost. I knew in my desperation to fit in and be accepted, I gradually needed to push my true self into the shadows, sacrificing my number one goal to gain approval of others who no longer hold any significance in my life. This decision, I now realise, was a complete disservice to myself; that is when I became a real loser. I know I'm not alone in this experience, and my mission is to ensure fewer people in the world go through the same struggle.

So, let's make a pact, for ourselves and for each other: it's okay to be different, to accept our uniqueness, and to take risks in pursuit of our goals. We must never allow others' opinions to define us or dictate our paths. Instead, let's strive to be the highest, truest versions of ourselves, and refuse to let anyone—especially ourselves—hold us back from achieving greatness. You have the power to choose your own pace and direction in your personal growth, and I'm here to support you on that journey. I've always felt a strong spiritual connection, especially as I've grown older, and I believe there's a reason you're reading this. I'm confident that the messages in this book will resonate with you, guiding you toward the best version of yourself. So, are you ready to take the first step?

Reading on, you'll discover that the power to achieve greatness lies within you, not in external factors. Regardless of your background, circumstances, or past experiences, you have the capability to define your path and persistently work towards your dreams.

Together, we'll go on a journey to unlock the tools necessary for personal growth. You'll cultivate self-awareness, recognise and face fear, develop resilience, and foster a growth mindset. By mastering these essential aspects of personal development and never giving up, you'll uncover your true potential and realise that anyone can achieve anything they set their mind to. Let's dive straight in.

"In every generation, we are all the chosen ones. Each of us has a unique purpose, a destiny waiting to be fulfilled. We possess the power and strength to make a difference in the world, to fight for what is right, and to bring about positive change. So, let us discover and accept our individual strengths and rally together as a united force, for the betterment of ourselves and the world around us." - M D Jenkins

Chapter 1

DISCOVERING WHO YOU ARE

Being very young is often considered a time in our lives when we are the most carefree and authentic with an open imagination of what is possible for us and it is often considered limitless. It's a period in time before society places expectations on us, responsibilities are handed out, and conformity in all situations shapes our understanding of who we are. As we grow older, we can lose touch with that authentic self, feeling like we are living a life that isn't truly connected to us.

I deeply feel we should all be living a life that is most connected to the essence of who we are as that is when we feel most alive and are able to give more, and with this, we receive more back. From my own personal experience going on the path of self-discovery begins with understanding that identity is not a fixed concept but rather a complex tapestry of beliefs, experiences, and emotions. Our life is often like a mirror, reflecting back to us what we are, expressed through our thoughts, feelings and actions. Knowing who we are can help reflect back what we truly want and desire in our lives. We should aim to dive deep within ourselves to uncover our true desires, free from societal expectations or conventional gender norms, knowing that we all possess unique characteristics and, in the understanding, that individuality is 100% the key to a successful life.

Societal norms often force restrictive gender roles and expectations that may hinder our authentic self-expression. The best way in discovering who we are outside of these norms is to challenge the expectations set upon us, question their origins, and free ourselves from the constraints they impose. Recognising that the 'true you' is not limited by any preconceived notions of masculinity or femininity. This may sound more difficult than it actually is, true expression is just beyond the fear of judgement and challenging the need to fit in.

ACCEPTANCE

In recent years, conversations surrounding identity have become increasingly prevalent, with individuals navigating the personal and political dimensions of finding labels that resonate with their inner selves. Throughout my life, I've embraced my identity as a man and have always been secure in that knowledge. At the same time, I've found myself drawn to the stories of female characters and their unique journeys. Even as a young boy, I was fascinated by their experiences and perspectives.

This interest has enriched my understanding of the world and deepened my empathy for the diverse paths we all walk in life. While I know who I am in my own identity, I also recognise and respect the importance of embracing the stories and experiences of others, and I celebrate the rich variety of human experiences that surrounds us.

My interest in this was an incredibly difficult feeling for me to handle growing up in a time when boys were supposed to be seen as tough and not show any interest in things considered feminine or associated with girls. However, I couldn't help it, despite some of my interests being in stereotypical 'boys' activities, I also loved a lot of stereotypical 'girly' things too and it seemed linked to my unique identity. Buffy, which has now been regarded as one of the best TV series of all time by many publications, was my absolute childhood hero. I found the character of Buffy to be both inspiring and relatable to me. Buffy was a character that broke gender stereotypes in many ways and I loved her for it.

Firstly, Buffy was a physically strong and capable fighter, a role that is often linked with male characters and seeing it in a female form amazed me and resonated with me. The fact she was this powerful and skilled fighter, challenged the traditional idea that women are weak and need protection, and instead showcases female strength and power and that was it, I was fascinated. She possessed qualities I admired such as bravery and leadership skills but despite enormous strength and responsibility; she was loving, kind, cared about her appearance and was able to show her vulnerability throughout the show. This helped me on my journey of being able to navigate my own roles and identities.

Secondly, Buffy was a character who was not defined solely by her relationships. Instead, she navigated her own personal and professional challenges, and prioritised her own needs and goals. Buffy deeply loved throughout the time on the show but knew that she was capable without the relationship and to me I always thought it was a brilliant mindset to have.

Discovering that Buffy, despite being a strong female character with masculine traits, did not lose her femininity was a pivotal moment for me. It taught me a powerful lesson in self-acceptance and authenticity. As a man with some stereotypical feminine traits, I struggled with feeling like I didn't quite fit in. But Buffy's example helped me realise that being true to myself, no matter how I expressed my gender, was what really mattered. I learned that all aspects of myself were valuable and worthy of acceptance. By accepting both my masculine and feminine traits, I became the complete version of myself and learned to thrive in the knowing, they were both a part of me and that is okay.

Recognising and embracing others' unique identities is an essential part of nurturing our self-development. Support the beauty of diversity, understanding that every individual's journey is worthy of respect and acceptance. By cultivating a space of inclusivity, we create a supportive environment that celebrates and nurtures the exploration of self-identity. As you go along your unique journey of self-discovery, do remember that your experiences have the power to inspire and empower others. Everybody has a different perception of themselves and if we uplift and support those we come into contact with, we may change a negative experience for someone else in a positive one, that is what I call *powerful influence*.

When we use this powerful influence to inspire and empower others, we not only make a positive impact on their lives, but we also discover a deeper sense of purpose and fulfilment within ourselves. Our actions have the ability to change someone's perception of themselves and the world around them. Through supporting and uplifting those around us, we not only create a ripple effect of positivity, but we also begin to see our own strengths and values in a clearer light. We realise the immense power we hold within ourselves to be a force for good in the world. It is in the giving and service to others that we receive the greatest reward of all - a deeper understanding of who we are and our unique place in this world. So, let us be conscious of the effect we have on those around us and strive to use our power to inspire and uplift, for in doing so, we not only help others to discover their true potential, but we also unlock the true potential within ourselves. And that's for real.

Accepting the idea that self-discovery is a journey of breaking free from the mould and embracing your own personal, fluid understanding of what it means to be 'you' is so impactful. Taking control of our story is one of those paths we must take in order to experience true empowerment and fulfilment in our lives. We can embrace the capability to rewrite the script of our life at any point, as we are always in control of our decisions, no matter the circumstances. Take this from me, use your own researched understanding of self-identity to redefine your narrative, shaping your experiences and interactions in a way that aligns with your authentic self. Reject any attempts to confine you within stereotypes, and celebrate the diverse expressions that exist within you and around you.

This is most definitely a 'shoulda, woulda, coulda' situation but if I had not listened to the noise of others trying to dim my light and fully accepted myself, my life may have turned out differently, perhaps filled with more joy and fulfilment much earlier. But instead, I let the opinions and judgments of others weigh me down, causing me to doubt myself and hold back from pursuing my true passions and aspirations.

Looking back, I realise that I take full responsibility for not fully backing who I am and all that I am capable of achieving. However, this realisation has also given me the motivation and courage to let go of the past and start living my life on my own terms, regardless of what others may think or say.

When considering finding our true purpose and what this means for us, it can be one of life's most daunting tasks, but one of the most important steps towards this process is having that full self-acceptance. Accepting ourselves for who we are, flaws and all, allows us to let go of any preconceived notions or expectations we may have been tightly holding onto.

When we learn to champion ourselves, we open up to the potential of discovering our true passions, talents, and unique qualities that make us stand out from all others. By allowing ourselves to be freely ourselves, we release any hindrances to discovering our true calling and finding meaning in our lives. Self-acceptance can unlock many doors to personal growth and opportunities to finding our own unique purpose. So, a message to you, be truthful but kind to yourself and create this journey by welcoming everything that makes you, you.

Meditation

Meditation is a practice that has been around for centuries, originating from ancient civilisations such as India and China. It has been used as a tool for both spiritual and psychological growth, as well as for exploring the deeper aspects of the self. Over time, meditation techniques have evolved and have been shaped by various religious and philosophical practices.

So, what exactly is meditation? At its core, meditation involves focusing our attention on a particular object, thought, or activity. This could range from focusing on the breath, repeating a mantra, or visualising a peaceful scene. The goal is to quiet the mind and become more present in the moment, allowing for a greater sense of inner calm and clarity and for me was not the easiest thing in the world to do.

As I sat cross-legged on my meditation/yoga mat, I couldn't escape the continuous chatter in my mind. Thoughts raced through my head, one after another, distracting me from the present moment mainly because my back seemed to hurt from sitting upright. It was a battle to stay still, to resist the temptation of checking my phone or just simply giving up altogether and heaven forbid, watch TV. I struggled to be with myself, to appreciate and accept who I was without relying on distractions.

I needed to create a guide for myself to overcome the distractions and learn to be present with myself even it is was for 10 minutes a day. I will share what I did with you:

- **I set a clear intention**: Before starting my meditation session, I spoke out loud to myself what my purpose of today's meditation was and set an intention. When I had a particularly hard day at work, I practiced this:

- **Purpose**: To release the stress and tension from a challenging day at work.
- **Intention**: "I intend to let go of the day's difficulties, to relax my body and mind, and to find a sense of renewal and rejuvenation through todays meditation practice as I deserve it."

    This helped me stay focused during the session, the scrambling thoughts became less.

- **I choose a quiet environment**: Finding a peaceful and distraction-free space for my meditation practice was always hard, I tried everywhere. The bath was the only place I didn't feel like running away, so the bath is where I would go.

- **Focused on my breath**: As I begin meditating, I would bring my attention to my breath. I began to actually notice the sensation of air moving in and out of my body. This served me well as a novice to keep my mind grounded.

- **Observed my thoughts**: When scrambling, distracting thoughts came up, I acknowledged them without judgment. Imagined them as cars passing by, looking on from the side of the road. This mindfulness practice helped me detach from continuous thoughts, giving them less weight and helped maintain focus.

- **Returned to my breath**: Once I acknowledged any distracting thoughts, I would slowly redirect my attention back to my breath. This really helped in strengthening my ability to let go of any distractions.

- **Practice self-compassion**: I used to get so frustrated with myself during the process. Recognising that distractions are natural and part of the meditation experience and everything needs time to elevate.
- **Consistent practice**: Regular meditation practice helped me to become more skilled at handling those distractions and maintaining focus. Dedicating time daily for my meditation sessions ensured I would get the true benefits.

Throughout my experience with meditation, I discovered it was in this quiet stillness that I was able to discover who I truly was, my passions, my desires, and my strengths. And from this newfound understanding, I was able to come to a place of acceptance and love for myself. It wasn't easy and sometimes it still isn't, but it is worth it. And I know that if I can do it, so can others. Meditation is a powerful tool, one that can help you discover who you truly are and come to a peaceful place with yourself.

From my experience one of the most significant benefits of meditation is that it can help us become more in tune with ourselves and our inner essence. By learning to quiet the mind like I have been practising and becoming more present, we can more readily connect with our true selves and gain a greater understanding of our thoughts, emotions, and desires.

Meditation can also help us become more present in our daily lives. Often, we are so consumed by our thoughts of the past and worries of the future that we are not fully present in the moment. We may be physically present, but our minds are elsewhere. Through regular meditation practice I have found we can train ourselves to be more mindful and present, allowing us to fully appreciate and engage in the world around us.

I strongly believe that meditation is a powerful tool for self-discovery and personal growth. It allows us to connect with our inner selves, become more present in the moment, and cultivate a greater sense of inner peace and harmony. I have realised even if I feel it should be, I know it is not for everybody but if you ever feel you are looking to explore the deeper aspects of yourself or even reduce a little bit of stress from the day, meditation is a practice that can really benefit. So, take a long deep breath, silence your mind, and let yourself be fully present in the moment. You may just be surprised at what you discover.

"You are too concerned about what was and what will be. There is a saying: yesterday is history, tomorrow is a mystery, but today is a gift. That is why it is called the present." - Master Oogway, Kung Fu Panda.

Success Journey

Self-discovery is a crucial step in our 'success journey', particularly when it comes to our career and financial stability. It is all too comfortable to get stuck in a job or pursuit that may not align with our values, personality, or skills, leading to low job satisfaction and lack of overall financial success. This is because we tend to take a job just for the money so we can spend that money on trying to impress those around us, who are actually just doing the same thing too.

Knowing who we are and what we want out of life is vital in order to make informed and confident decisions regarding our career paths. When we truly understand our strengths, values, passions, and goals, we are better equipped to choose professions or businesses that align with our aspirations and help us achieve our professional goals.

Conversely, those who lack a sense of who they are or who they would like to be may struggle to make meaningful connections with their work and fail to find satisfaction in their careers. By exploring our inner selves, we can gain a deeper understanding of our personal and professional identities, which can drive us towards success and accomplishment in our careers. Therefore, taking the necessary steps towards self-discovery can help us unlock our full potential and attain the career and financial success we truly desire.

To discover our ideal career path, we would need to take an introspective look at ourselves to understand our personality traits, values, and skills we can expand on. This can be achieved by reflecting on past experiences, examining our strengths and weaknesses, and perhaps undergoing personality tests.

I did a personality test called 16 personalities and what it suggested to me was that my personality is described as an 'Advocate (INFJ-A)'. The results of the test told me I had a unique set of personality traits that makes me intuitive, empathetic, and compassionate. In terms of self-discovery, these qualities help me to gain a deeper understanding of myself and others. My intuition allows you to pick up on subtle cues and feelings that others may not be aware of, helping me to develop a greater awareness of my own emotions and needs.

Additionally, my empathy and compassion can help you to develop a greater sense of understanding towards yourself. By embracing these qualities, I can use my innate sense of intuition and empathy to uncover my passions, purpose, and inner strengths, leading to a more fulfilled and purpose-driven life. The results of the test are qualities I see in myself and even though like everyone, I am a lot more complicated, I believe those qualities help me reach out in the best way to fulfil my purpose of helping others in my career and life.

What personality are you? If you would like to take the test to discover a little bit more about you, go to the website - www.16personalities.com.

For financial success, self-discovery plays a crucial role in understanding our financial beliefs, habits, and attitudes towards saving and investing. A person who grew up in a family that constantly struggled with their finances may have heard things such as 'money doesn't come easy or it doesn't grow on trees', this can increase the chances of developing a scarcity mindset, meaning they are left with a feeling or belief there is never enough or that rich people are greedy people who have taken it all for themselves.

This can lead to misguided spending habits and the inability to save or invest. Through self-discovery exercises such as journaling, affirmations, and learning about personal finance, a person can change their money beliefs and adopt healthy financial habits that lead to a better chance of financial success.

As you choose to launch into your journey towards self-discovery, always remember that you hold the power to create a life that suits you both professionally and personally. Exploring your true passions, values, and beliefs will absolutely guide you towards the path that resonates with your soul.

However, achieving career and financial satisfaction doesn't necessarily mean you have to leave or quit your job right away or at all, as you can also work towards something that brings you joy on the side through side hustles or flexible work environments. Finding this balance is key to achieving your definition of a "rich life." So, as you take steps towards achieving success, remember to prioritise your passions and your own well-being. Ask yourself, "What does my rich life look like?" and take the leap towards creating your own unique and fulfilling career and life.

Relationships

We will speak more about building positive relationships later on in the chapters to come but discovering who you are is a critical step in building healthy relationships and friendships. When you know yourself, you can understand your needs, values, and boundaries. This self-knowledge helps you make better choices in your relationships. It enables you to communicate more effectively with others about what you want and need in a friendship or romantic relationship.

In my own personal life, I have battled a lot throughout the years with myself about people-pleasing and prioritising others' needs over my own. I often felt resentful when my friends, family or partners didn't show me the same level of consideration. This expectation caused a great deal of broken communication and a struggle to keep certain relationships consistent. It wasn't until I took the time to examine my own values and priorities that I realised my behaviour was rooted in a fear of rejection and a need for external validation. Once I began to acknowledge my own needs and establish healthy boundaries, my relationships improved dramatically with the right people. I am now more vocal with the word 'No' when I truly do not want to give my energy to something so then when I do say 'Yes' I am able to show up as my authentic self in all of my relationships. By putting my own needs first, I am now able to give more to those around me without resentment or expectation which I have to say, feels so good.

The journey of self-discovery is ongoing, and it is essential as we discussed to approach it with compassion and self-acceptance. Once you begin to know and love yourself fully, you can form deeper connections with others and build relationships rooted in mutual trust and respect. Remember, the most fulfilling relationships are those where both parties show up as themselves genuinely and are able to communicate honestly and openly.

To sum up, discovering who you are is the foundation upon which you can build a rewarding and authentic life. From examining your individual identity and relationship dynamics to navigating career and money decisions, self-knowledge can be such a powerful tool. By understanding your personal values, strengths, and boundaries, you can navigate gender norms and societal expectations with confidence and clarity. You can cultivate enjoyable relationships and build a supportive community of love around you. With all this knowledge, you can confidently map out your career and financial plans that are aligned with your personal values and goals. The world is wide open for you, if you are wide open to it.

Keep this in mind, everyone is unique, and the journey of self-discovery is individualised so take that time for self-reflection, and mindfulness even if you have to meditate on it. Don't shy from seeking guidance and support from friends, family, or professionals as you go through your journey. Fall in love with your individuality, challenge those societal norms, and open yourself up to new perspectives. By discovering who you are, you can live a life of integrity and purpose, and that is truly a life worth living.

TASK

It is now the time to dig deep and discover who you truly are. By following these seven simple steps, you can venture into a transformative journey of self-discovery, uncovering your values, strengths, and greatest desires. From setting aside time for self-reflection to committing to taking action, this could be helpful for you to take the first steps towards unlocking your full potential. So, like in meditation, take a deep breath, and let's get started.

Step #1: Start by setting aside some time on your calendar for self-reflection. Write it on there, whether it's a single afternoon or a week-long retreat, make sure that you give yourself the space to delve deep into your psyche and uncover your true self.

Step #2: Once you've carved out some time, begin to think the big questions.

What do I like about myself?
What do I stand for?
What are my core values?
What am I really good at?
What could I work on or like to be better at?

Step #3: Take five minutes to free-write your answers to these questions. This exercise is all about being honest and genuine with yourself, so don't hold back.

Step #4: Once you've answered these big questions, it's time to get specific. Take a look at four key areas of your life – money, career, relationships, and identity – and ask yourself what **YOU** really want from each of these areas.

Step #5: Again, take five minutes to free-write your answers to each of these questions. Don't be afraid to dream big and aim high. Think BIG but stay true to you.

Step #6: With your answers in hand, start to think about how you can align them with your values, strengths, and desires.

What changes need to be made?
What steps can you take to make those changes happen?

Write down a specific first action for each area.

Step #7: The final step is to commit to taking action. Don't let this exercise be a one-time event, come back to it as you'll discover more as you read on. Use it as a guide for ongoing self-discovery and personal growth. Regularly take stock of your progress, and adjust your course as necessary. Remember, life is unpredictable, but with these tools in hand, you can keep moving forward and living your best life.

By following this task, you will gain clarity about your values, desires, strengths, and weaknesses. You'll learn what you want from life and how to align your actions with your goals. This, in turn, can help you improve your life in areas such as money, career, relationships, friendships, and identity.

There is some space to write but if you have a journal or notepad, you can use this.

Chapter 2

SELF-AWARENESS

Ever wondered why some people are able to navigate life's challenges with grace and grow from their experiences? The key lies in self-awareness— understanding your thoughts, feelings, and behaviour patterns. Self-awareness is like having a personal GPS installed that helps you identify your strengths, acknowledge your weaknesses, and steer you towards better decisions.

But self-awareness isn't just about personal growth; it also enhances your relationships. By becoming more attuned to your emotions, you'll develop empathy for others' perspectives and forge stronger, more meaningful connections. Ultimately, self-awareness is the game-changer that can transform your life, both personally and professionally.

Without self-awareness, you may end up living a life that does not reflect your true self. It is easy to lose oneself in the crowd and suppress your thoughts, emotions, and actions to fit in with everyone else. By doing this, you will lose touch with your true identity, causing feelings of loneliness and disconnection. You may also experience low self-esteem that makes it difficult to express yourself and can damage your emotional and mental health.

As I know from personal experience, losing self-awareness is like continuously walking in someone else's shadow. I used to hide and withdraw in my younger years because I was desperate to fit in with everyone else, and I didn't want to accept who I was, this meant I tried my hardest to act in a persona for many years of my life. This led me to disconnect with my own feelings, style, and opinions. I became a follower who just did what everyone else was doing without considering my own beliefs first.

It wasn't until I chose to break away from the crowd and rediscover my authentic self that I began to truly thrive. Self-awareness allowed me to gain confidence in my own decisions, rediscover my passions, and rebuild meaningful connections with those around me. In recognising and accepting my strengths and weaknesses, I was able to develop my skills and pursue my goals with a clearer head.

Everyone has exceptional skills, talents, and perspectives inside of them that they can bring to any team or environment. By getting to know who we truly are and cultivating self-awareness, we can recognise what we bring to the table and contribute to a greater purpose. There is power in allowing your true self to surface, and it can result in profound personal growth and satisfaction.

"I believe everyone in the world is born with genius-level talent. Apply yourself to whatever you're genius at, and you can do anything in the world." – Jay Z

Have you ever made a decision that left you feeling embarrassed and ashamed? Like you were not truly in tune with your thoughts, emotions, and actions? Perhaps you were simply searching for a way to be noticed and acknowledged by others. I have been there too and I'm glad I learned from it.

One particular experience that comes to mind is when I attended a birthday party back in my teens and ended up ruining the night for the host by punching holes in a dry wall in stupidity, simply just to be noticed for doing it. In hindsight, I realised that my actions were not rational nor aligned with who I truly wanted to be. I had distanced myself from my own identity in order to fit in or be seen by others. But in doing so, I ended up feeling ashamed and like I had made a big mistake.

Making silly mistakes just to get noticed by people who don't care about you is one of the biggest roadblocks on your journey towards self-awareness. In fact, it is nothing but a waste of your precious time and energy, believe me I know. Every single second of your life is too valuable to be wasted in trying to impress people who don't matter or who won't add anything meaningful to your life. As a result, you end up diminishing your sense of self-worth and lowering your own self-esteem, allow your light to shine bright.

Remember, self-awareness is all about discovering and accepting your own unique strengths and weaknesses so that means not having to seek validation or approval from others, how liberating is that?! So, don't make the decision to let anyone else define your worth. Instead, focus on becoming the best version of yourself and let the world take notice of your self-growth and achievements.

So, ask yourself, have you ever had an experience that made you question where you're going in life? An experience that forced you to ask yourself tough questions about where you may be going wrong and how to fix it? For me, that experience at the party was a catalyst for self-awareness and reflection. It made me realise how crucial it is to examine our inner selves, understand our subconscious thoughts and emotions, and uncover who we are and who we truly want to be.

Taking accountability

This is something I used to shy away from as it was too uncomfortable to talk about as it meant staring at yourself in the mirror, it's time to get real about accountability. Let me tell you, this stuff is life-changing. Back in the day, I was a pro at shifting blame, it was never but life had other plans for me.

So, there I was, late for to pick my cousin up from the airport because of a flat tire. Of course, my go-to reaction was to blame the potholes, the person who didn't indicate, the council, the government or even the universe itself. But then it hit me – maybe if I had checked my tire pressure before a long journey or even regularly, I wouldn't be in this mess. That's when I realised that taking accountability for my own actions could transform my life.

Here's the deal: accountability is like being out in the rain with no umbrella. Without it, you're going to get wet, meaning you're going to experience setbacks and obstacles in life. With preparation, you can avoid these but if you don't, remember it's on you!

When you practice accountability, you're not only building trust with others but also with yourself. Every time you follow through with your commitments, you prove to yourself that you're reliable and dependable. This self-trust is a powerful tool for personal growth and empowerment.

On the flip side, when you don't keep your promises to yourself, you're the only one to blame. This realisation can be so uncomfortable, but it's also liberating because it puts the power to change back in your hands.

One of the most exciting aspects of taking full responsibility for your actions is that you get to claim your wins and triumphs as your own. When you achieve success, it's because of your hard work, determination, and accountability. This sense of ownership over your achievements can be incredibly motivating and inspiring.

Now, I know what you're thinking, "But accountability sounds hard!" And yeah, it can be. But when those wins come it's worth it!

Self-Sabotagery

Have you ever found yourself on the brink of success, only to think, no, something bad will happen, this won't work out and ultimately fall short of your goal? You may be experiencing what I call, self-sabotagery —the act of subconsciously undermining your personal progress. Often, this behaviour stems from a fear of displacement, as success can sometimes feel like it separates us from our loved ones and our roots. By understanding these patterns, you can break free from limiting behaviours and thrive to your full capacity.

Identifying Self-Sabotagery

Self-sabotagery refers to the seemingly counterproductive actions we take that hold us back from achieving our goals. It manifests in various aspects of life, such as career, relationships, and personal growth. Examples include procrastination, engaging in toxic relationships, and neglecting health and wellness.

The fear of displacement can be a key driver of self-sabotaging behaviour. We worry that success might distance us from friends and family, disrupting the familiar comfort of our social circle. Recognising these patterns is crucial to overcoming them.

Acknowledging the Fear of Displacement

The fear of displacement arises from the anxiety that personal growth and success might change the relationships around us, making us feel isolated or misunderstood. This fear can originate in a desire to maintain a sense of belonging and a worry of being perceived as superior or different from the people we love and grew up with.

Consider Anna, who grew up in a tight-knit family with extremely modest means. As she climbed the ladder in her work life, her salary and status became higher than her family had ever seen. Her family were proud of her but all she heard was "I couldn't never do your job, it's so stressful, I don't know why you put yourself through it". These remarks made Anna feel guilty about her newfound success and feared that her family would view her as "too good for them." As a result, Anna began neglecting her career goals as time went on, she felt increasingly disconnected from her family.

Cultivating Self-Awareness to Overcome Self-Sabotagery

Self-awareness is crucial in recognising self-sabotaging thoughts and behaviours. By understanding your triggers and emotional responses, you can better navigate situations that might lead to self-sabotagery.

Strategies to Overcome Self-Sabotagery

Addressing the fear of displacement and overcoming self-sabotagery requires reframing your perspective and communicating openly with loved ones. Here are some tips

Reframe negative thoughts and beliefs:

Replace limiting beliefs about success and relationships with positive affirmations that emphasise that you can have huge potential for personal growth and also have deepening connections with loved ones.

Communicate openly with friends and family:

Share your goals and aspirations with loved ones, explaining that your pursuit of success is motivated by the desire for personal growth and a better future for everyone.

Find a support system:

Surround yourself with people who encourage personal growth and success while maintaining authentic relationships. Join a mastermind group, attend networking events, or connect with mentors who can offer guidance and support.

Self-sabotagery can be a significant roadblock to personal growth, but by recognising its connection to the fear of displacement, you can take proactive steps to overcome it. Cultivate self-awareness, reframe your perspective, communicate openly with loved ones, and find a supportive community. Remember, authentic relationships and success are not mutually exclusive— you can have both.

JOURNALING

Through journaling, I created a journey of self-discovery, and it was deeply empowering. I become more self-aware and was able to gain a clearer understanding of my triggers and behaviours. This practice of self-reflection can be hard, but it helps us explore our deeper selves and allows us to develop the skills to overcome the obstacles that hinder us from our true potential.

Additionally, journaling helped me identify both my strengths and weaknesses, paving the way for me to begin the journey of creating the best version of myself. I learned that my strengths included being helpful, insightful and always being there for those I love in need, while my weaknesses had a direct influence on my ability to develop certain areas of my life further.

Putting my thoughts down on paper provided clarity, which made me recognise certain patterns and behaviours that I had previously not been aware of, empowering me to act in a more aligned way with my values and beliefs. In turn, developing a greater sense of self-awareness allowed me to make better decisions and reflect on those I had already made. This practice has not only reduced my stress and anxiety levels but has also ensured that I am taking the necessary steps to create the life I desire.

One time in my life that again, journaling really helped me was when my partner started a business that quickly grew a big online following in a niche industry, attracting haters and trolls. They propagated false and damaging stories that impugned both my partner's business success and our personal lives. The experience overwhelmed us and we felt hurt and frustrated with the negativity and false narratives. But journaling helped me process those feelings, manage stress and prevent spiralling into despair. By focusing on the positive impact, we had made in the lives of our true supporters, we ignored the negativity and concentrated all the more on our kinder relationships.

In summary, journaling has become my go-to tool to stay grounded, manage my emotions, and gain a clarity and understanding about myself and what direction I needed to take in life.

"Journal writing gives us insights into who we are, who we were, and who we can become." - Sandra Marinella

There is a famous study by conducted by James Pennebaker and his colleagues at the University of Texas at Austin in the late 1980s and early 1990s to show that young people who journal are better able to manage their emotions and stress. Just starting out and discovering adult life is tough. It can be overwhelming to manage finances, build relationships, and navigate career paths. Journaling has been proven to help manage this, mainly because the tough times don't have to stay locked in your head, they can exit onto paper or in any healthy, positive expression. This study did resonate personally with me as journaling has continued to be a helpful tool for me in my personal growth journey and one that is now a habit and I will use throughout my life.

Setting aside time to write has helped me to process and express my emotions in a constructive way. It has helped me to identify areas where I can improve, such as managing my stress levels and developing better coping mechanisms. It has also allowed me to keep track of my progress and celebrate my successes. As I said before, it has helped me to become more conscious and reflective of my thoughts and feelings. It is a great way to cope with difficult situations and to gain insight into yourself.

Self-awareness is the bridge between who we are and who we want to be. As we've discussed, it's the ability to understand our thoughts, emotions and habits and how they impact our lives.

During my journey of self-discovery, I grappled with a growing dependence on cannabis. Initially, it served as a casual pastime in my 20s, but soon transformed into a daily habit that began I believe to undermine my potential. While it did, in my mind, spark occasional bursts of creativity, I found myself increasingly unambitious, afraid to venture out of my comfort zone and explore opportunities beyond my immediate surroundings. My mind felt clouded, and inspiration was scarce.

I began turning down invitations to social events, cutting myself off from the chance to build connections and nurture personal growth. The habit became a hindrance, and I realised it was time to make a change. With newfound determination, I made the decision to quit.

The mental clarity I gained was astounding, allowing me to see life through fresh eyes, brimming with opportunities and possibilities. No longer held captive by my habit, I felt a renewed sense of freedom and purpose. It's important to note that this experience isn't meant to condemn cannabis entirely, as I understand its effects can vary from person to person. However, in my case, the habit was negatively affecting my ambition and well-being.

Looking back, I recognise the crucial role self-awareness played in my transformation. By acknowledging my habits and understanding their impact on my life, I was able to foster personal growth. Quitting wasn't easy, but the rewards were immeasurable.

My experience has taught me the importance of balance in life. While it's okay to explore and have fun, it's equally essential to maintain awareness of our habits and ensure they don't become detrimental to our goals and well-being. Self-awareness is key to finding that equilibrium.

I share my story in the hope that it resonates with others who may be facing similar struggles. By embracing self-awareness and being open to change, we can break free from the shackles of our habits and embark on a journey towards personal growth and fulfilment.

Self-awareness is one of the most powerful tools that can help you tap into your intuition and lead a more fulfilling life. It helps us to understand our habits, emotions, and thoughts, and to identify the ones that are serving us, and the ones that aren't. By practicing self-awareness, we can create a life that aligns with our truest selves, and move towards our goals and dreams with clarity and purpose. We all have the potential to dream big, but we first need to be aware of the habits and patterns that may be holding us back. Once we have that awareness, we can take the necessary steps to break free and create a life of our choosing.

By becoming more in tune with your thoughts and feelings, you can learn to listen to the little voice of intuition that guides you in the right direction. Whether you're facing a major life decision or simply need to make a choice in the moment, your intuition can help you make the best choice for your unique situation. By practicing mindfulness and self-reflection, you can begin to recognise the subtle messages your intuition is sending you.

Once you've learned to listen to your intuition, you can use it to navigate life's challenges with greater ease and confidence. With self-awareness as your guide, you can encourage your inner strength and wisdom to make the decisions that best serve you and lead you towards your path of success and satisfaction. So, I ask you, are you ready to take your first step if you haven't already, towards greater self-awareness and self-development?

Steven's story: Money or Fulfilment? How about both?

A lot of people find themselves constantly questioning their career path, feeling unfulfilled, and yearning for something more meaningful! Steven had been in the same position for years until he listened to his intuition and took a leap of faith.

Steven had secured a senior position in a company and had been working there for several years. He was extremely knowledgeable, hard-working and was considered a vital part of the team. However, he always felt like something was missing. He would always mention he was only doing his job for the above-average salary, and there was no real sense of personal fulfilment in his work.

Steven began to engage in conversations about the pursuit of something more meaningful. One day, Steven was convinced of an idea that he slept on for several days. The idea was completely unrelated to his current job role, but the more he thought about it, the more he felt a pull towards it.

At first, Steven tried to ignore his intuition and pushed the idea aside, thinking that it was too risky to leave his stable job for an opportunity to build something of his own. However, the little voice inside him kept urging him to go ahead with the idea. Gradually, he began to reflect on his career goals and recognised that he wasn't happy with his current situation, and the vision he had aligned better with his interests and values.

With newfound self-awareness and courage, Steven decided to listen to his intuition and develop his idea further. To his surprise, the project took off, thrived, and made him more money than before. But more importantly, Steven was feeling more fulfilled than ever before.

Through this experience, Steven learned the power of listening to his intuition and following his heart, discovering how important self-awareness is in making important decisions. He found the courage to pursue his dreams, and that is something truly remarkable.

So, if you find yourself in a situation similar to Steven's, feeling unfulfilled and questioning your career, I urge you to start listening to your intuition. Reflect on your goals and values, and start taking small steps towards pursuing something more meaningful to you. Remember, life is too short to be unhappy in your work, and there's no better time than now to start living in your fulfilment and earning money in something you truly love.

TASK

We have discovered that self-awareness is a crucial aspect of personal development. It helps you understand your strengths and weaknesses, beliefs and values, emotions, and patterns of behaviour. It enables you to identify and change negative patterns and behaviours while enhancing positive aspects of yourself. By improving your self-awareness, you can discover your true self, which can lead to better decision-making, a more fulfilling life, and improved relationships with others.

In this six-step adventure, we'll explore practical strategies to boost self-awareness and embrace the best version of ourselves.

Step #1: Strengths and Weaknesses - Knowing ourselves

Begin by making a list of your strengths and weaknesses. Be honest and kind to yourself – we all have areas to celebrate and improve upon. This inventory helps us appreciate our unique qualities and identify opportunities for growth.

Step #2: Beliefs and Values - Discover Your Inner Compass

Understanding our core beliefs and values is crucial for navigating life with purpose and authenticity. Ask yourself, "What do I believe in? What's truly important to me?" These insights when written down guide us towards making decisions aligned with our true selves.

Step #3: Mindfulness - Be Present and Aware

Practicing mindfulness helps us stay in the present moment and become more aware of our thoughts, feelings, and behaviours. Start with 10-15 minutes of daily mindfulness meditation. Focus on your breath and observe your inner experiences with compassion.

Step #4: Emotional Reflection - Feelings as Teachers

Emotions are essential aspects of our lives, offering valuable insights into our experiences. Take time to reflect on your emotions, journal your thoughts, and seek to understand their deeper meanings. Embracing our feelings nurtures self-awareness and emotional resilience.

Step #5: Past Lessons - Grow Through Experience

Looking back on past experiences reveals patterns and lessons that shape who we are today. Consider what you've learned and how it influences your current behaviour. By understanding our history, we can better navigate the present and future.

Step #6: Action Plan - Chart Your Course

Using your newfound self-awareness, create an action plan to leverage your strengths, address areas for growth, and align your life with your values. Set achievable goals and celebrate your progress as you journey towards your best self.

Self-awareness is a lifelong journey that unfolds with patience, curiosity, and kindness. Remember even the hard moments is the process and learn to appreciate the unique person you are becoming.

Use the space below or your own journal for this task.

....

....

....

....

....

....

....

....

....

....

....

....

....

....

....

....

Chapter 3

OVERCOMING ANXIETY AND FACING FEAR

The comfort zone is a deceptive refuge, providing a seemingly safe space while allowing fear and anxiety to taunt you into believing it's where you belong. My heart raced as I denied my mum's suggestion to attend a university further from home, a choice I stubbornly clung to despite the lingering question of how that experience might have shaped my life differently. Although I don't necessarily regret my decision, the unresolved "what-if" serves as a constant reminder that overcoming fear and anxiety can lead to life-altering opportunities for growth and self-discovery.

Mental health is a topic that has been brought up more often in recent years, as we collectively work towards removing the stigma surrounding it, saving countless lives in the process. Increased awareness and education on the importance of mental wellbeing have made this progress possible. Back in the early 2000s, when I was at school, mental health was rarely, if at all, discussed, and it was something that was often swept under the rug. It brings me great joy to see that open conversations are now taking place, help is widely available, and people—especially the younger generation—are starting to recognise that seeking help is a strength, and they deserve to receive the support they need.

Having overcome mental health challenges myself, I hold a deep interest in helping others navigate similar struggles. Through my personal experiences and research, I have gained insights that may be relevant to your mental health journey.

As a child, I possessed an unexplainable yet remarkable ability to sense my mother's sadness and anxiety. Her battles with self-confidence and weight issues caused her immense pain, often consuming her. All I wanted was to help her feel better, to bring a smile to her face, and celebrate her victories. It was this selfless desire to ease my mother's pain that planted the seed of my passion for uplifting others.

On my journey of personal growth and self-discovery, I came to acknowledge the universal struggles and challenges we all face in life. Mental health issues, such as anxiety and depression, can leave us feeling overwhelmed and lost. Learning to develop a positive mindset is essential for facing these challenges head-on and overcoming the mental hurdles that hold us back.

Witnessing my mother's journey to self-confidence and happiness was a turning point for me. Watching her persistence and hard work help her find peace and joy in her life was truly inspirational. Her unwavering support and love for me throughout my life continue to be a driving force in everything I do.

The journey of self-help and self-discovery is profoundly transformative. It is akin to therapy for the soul. In sharing my journey and the lessons I've learned, I hope to help others find the inner strength needed to overcome their mental health struggles. It is possible to break free from the grip of anxiety, fear, and depression, and live a life filled with happiness and success. Let this book be your guide to tapping into your inner strength and the power of your mind to overcome fear and anxiety, and live the life you truly deserve.

ANXIETY

Anxiety is a common struggle that many people face in their lives. It can be triggered by various factors, including genetics and environmental causes. In my personal development journey, I discovered that fear and anxiety, particularly in social situations, were the main issues I had to overcome. It has been an ongoing battle throughout my life.

For the longest time, caring about what others thought of me was a significant challenge I had to face. I used to believe that I needed to fit in and be accepted to be considered "normal." Over time, I learned valuable tools that helped me realise I didn't need to be like everyone else to be accepted. The key to building meaningful relationships with others was to be true to myself. Accepting who I was and acknowledging that it was okay to be different became crucial to my growth and success. However, it's important to note that this is a lifelong journey, and sometimes I find myself slipping backwards, having to push myself forward again.

Self-love played an essential role in my journey of self-acceptance. Initially, practicing self-love was quite challenging. But being able to look at yourself in the mirror and say, "I love you," can be one of the most liberating acts of self-love. When I first tried it, I felt silly and uncomfortable, but I kept doing it. I needed to

become accustomed to what I looked and sounded like, so I started talking more lovingly to myself.
Practicing self-love was vital to moving past my concerns about other people's opinions and focusing on myself. It took time, but like all habits, with practice, it became natural. It allowed me to build a stronger relationship with myself and become increasingly more confident in my skin.

I learned that people are not always thinking about me, and even if they did, they were too focused on their own issues to give me any serious thought. We cannot control what others think of us, but we can control what we think of ourselves. Self-love allowed me to be compassionate towards myself and others, making life easier and more enjoyable. It helped me become a much better version of myself and remember that everyone is on their unique journey.

Practicing self-love brought about a shift in my mindset and newfound confidence. It propelled me to begin accepting myself and become the person I wanted to be. This energy resonated with others in my life, and I attracted the right people at the right time. I no longer feel the need to hide or run away most of the time.

Remember that self-love is possible for everyone, and it can help you unlock your true potential. The journey to self-love may not be easy, but it is worth it. Practice self-love, be true to yourself, and trust that everything will fall in place. You will be amazed at the positive changes that can take place in your life.

According to my research, I'm not alone in my experiences. Fear and anxiety are extremely common mental health issues globally. The World Health Organisation (WHO) estimates that 264 million people worldwide suffer from anxiety disorders, making it the most prevalent mental health disorder globally.

My journey to mental wellness has been long and winding, but I'm proud of the progress I've made. Wherever you are in your journey, you should be proud of yourself too. I'm excited to share my story with you and hope it resonates with anyone who may be struggling. Together, we can create a kinder, more understanding world where everyone can thrive.

As our society evolves, we must acknowledge the significant progress made in self-expression. While social media has its drawbacks, platforms like TikTok have empowered people, particularly the youth, to showcase their true selves in unprecedented ways.

Authenticity lies at the heart of this movement. We no longer feel compelled to conceal our true selves, fostering deeper connections with those who share our interests and values. These connections are invaluable, especially regarding mental health.

Anxiety and depression can be isolating, but this era of openness offers hope and possibility. By embracing authenticity and forging supportive relationships, we can dismantle isolation and find the strength to overcome our struggles.

Openness can heal the wounds of past generations. Mental health has long been stigmatised and shrouded in shame. However, the more we openly discuss our struggles, the more we break down barriers and shift towards self-compassion.

By connecting with those who share our experiences, we find a sense of belonging and community. This connection can be profoundly healing for those who have felt alone or misunderstood. Empathy and understanding create a supportive network that fosters growth and well-being.

This era of authenticity presents a remarkable opportunity to move forward in our mental health journey. By embracing ourselves, cultivating meaningful connections, and practicing self-compassion, we can unlock new ways of thriving in the world.

Overcoming Anxiety

Having discussed the importance of self-acceptance and self-love in dealing with anxiety, we must now explore practical strategies to overcome it. Anxiety can be triggered by various factors, including genetics and environmental causes, and as we know now affects millions of people worldwide. In my journey, I discovered several tools and strategies that helped me navigate social situations and manage my anxiety.

Here are some strategies that have been instrumental in my personal development:

- **Mindfulness and Meditation**: For me, practicing mindfulness and meditation was initially a difficult endeavour. As someone who experiences anxiety, sitting still and focusing on the present moment seemed like an almost insurmountable task. However, with time and patience, I slowly began to develop a consistent meditation practice. Though it was challenging at first, I started to notice subtle changes in my mental state. I found myself better able to observe my thoughts without judgment and detach from the worries that once consumed me. The more I practiced, the more I realised the profound impact meditation had on reducing my anxiety. It's not always easy, but I'm grateful for the sense of calm and clarity that meditation brings to my life, and I continue to reap the benefits of this practice in managing my anxiety.

- **Physical Exercise**: When I first began putting exercise into my routine, it was an uphill battle. My anxiety was so overwhelming that during my first ever visit to a gym, I experienced a severe panic attack that left me catching my breath on the floor of the disabled toilet. It was a difficult moment, but I was determined to push through and not let anxiety hold me back. As I continued my journey with exercise, I discovered that it wasn't just the physical activity that challenged me but also the presence of others who seemed further along in their fitness journeys. My anxiety would spike when I compared myself to them, but over time, I learned to focus on my progress and celebrate my own successes.

  Through consistent practice, I began to build confidence, and gradually, the situations that once triggered my anxiety became more manageable. Today, exercise has become for me the most vital tool in managing my anxiety, and I've learned to welcome the challenges it presents, both physical and emotional. This journey has taught me resilience and self-belief, proving that facing my fears and committing to personal growth can yield incredible results.

- **Cognitive Behavioural Therapy (CBT)**: Although I haven't worked directly with a therapist, I've found that researching and applying CBT techniques has been immensely helpful in managing my anxiety. By learning to identify the negative thought patterns that fuel my anxiety, I've become more self-aware and better equipped to challenge these thoughts. Techniques such as reframing, mindfulness, and journaling have enabled me to develop healthier thinking habits and behaviours. As I've continued to practice these strategies, I've noticed a significant reduction in my anxiety levels and an increased sense of confidence in my ability to navigate life's challenges. The insights gained from researching CBT have empowered me to take control of my mental health and build a more positive, resilient mindset.

- **Healthy Lifestyle Choices**: Making a conscious effort to prioritise my well-being has played a significant role in reducing my anxiety. I've found that maintaining consistent sleep patterns has helped regulate my mood and improve my overall mental health. I strongly believe choosing a balanced diet has provided me with the nutrients and energy needed to face life's challenges with resilience. Moreover, my decision to give up smoking has not only alleviated anxiety but also improved my physical health.

  As much as I enjoy coffee, I've learned to limit my caffeine intake and found that doing so has decreased my anxiety levels. Lastly, by being mindful of my alcohol consumption, I've discovered that I'm better able to maintain a clear mind and navigate life's stressors more effectively. These changes have been instrumental in building a solid foundation for managing and overcoming anxiety.

- **Daily Gratitude:** Incorporating a daily gratitude practice has had a profound impact on managing my anxiety. By consciously focusing on the positive aspects of my life and expressing appreciation for them, I've gained valuable perspective. I have realised that many people around the world face much more significant challenges, such as highly stressful, fearful, and dangerous situations each day, this has helped me realise that my anxieties are often comparatively small. This shift in perspective has not only reduced my anxiety but also instilled a sense of gratitude for the blessings in my life. By acknowledging the hardships others endure, I've cultivated an appreciation for my own circumstances, which has created feelings of joy and fulfilment. Practicing gratitude has truly transformed my outlook and helped me manage anxiety with a newfound sense of empathy and understanding.

By adopting these strategies into my daily life, I was able to regain control and gain a sense of calm, even in the face of life's challenges. My hope is that by sharing these tools, you too can find relief and growth in your journey to overcome anxiety.

FEAR

Fear is an intriguing emotion that affects everyone at some point in their lives. It can hold us back from reaching our goals, prevent us from taking risks, and limit our potential. However, it's crucial to recognise that fear is entirely imaginary and originates in the mind.

Managing and facing our fears is essential for personal growth and success. Remember that fear is not reality, and we can move forward despite feeling scared. Taking action despite fear often leads to growth and success in every aspect of our lives.

Fear is what I call "wasted imagination." Our imagination is one of our most powerful gifts as humans, distinguishing us from other animals. It enables us to create our desired reality and go beyond mere survival to adapt and thrive. However, fear restricts our imagination by creating a mental block. Instead of using our imagination to find creative solutions to our problems, we focus on future stress and worry, leading back to anxiety. Recognising when fear holds us back and taking steps to overcome it is crucial.

Our imagination has led to extraordinary inventions and creations, providing us more time to pursue what we truly desire. These inventions have changed our lives and improved our quality of life. Imagination has allowed us to create technologies that bring us closer together and make life easier. It has enabled us to reach new heights and create a better world. It is a powerful tool that should be used to improve our world.

The reason we don't use our imagination more to enhance our lives and progress is that our brains are hard-wired to keep us safe. This made sense when our ancestors lived in the wild, and a Smilodon was making us lunch, but in today's world, it can leave us stuck in a cycle of fear and doubt. We must retrain our brains to trust in our creativity and potential to create a brighter future.

Using our imagination to push past our comfort zones transforms our lives and the world around us. We can't be held back by fear if we want to progress and reach our goals. Positive thinking and action are the only ways to create real change in our lives.

The key takeaway is that fear is entirely imaginary and holds no real power over us if we acknowledge this. We can harness our imagination to find creative solutions and push past our limitations. With the right mindset and positive action, anything is possible. Let's embrace our imagination and use it to build a better future for ourselves and the world.

Facing fear

Fear has been a part of my journey, and I've discovered some valuable strategies along the way to face it head on. In this chapter, I'll share the methods that have helped me face and conquer fear in my life. Here are the strategies that made a difference in my journey:

- **Self-Awareness:** My journey to facing fear has taught me the importance of self-awareness. By cultivating mindfulness and learning to recognise the moment fear arrives, I've been able to address it proactively. This heightened sense of awareness has enabled me to understand my emotions better and respond to them in healthier, more constructive ways. As I've become more attuned to my inner world, I've noticed a significant decrease in the power fear holds over me.

- **Challenging My Negative Thought Patterns**: I used to be held captive by my negative thoughts, constantly telling myself that I couldn't do something because of what others might think. But I've learned to challenge these thoughts and reframe my perspective. Now, instead of assuming the worst, I choose to assume the best outcome. By shifting my mindset to "they will love it, and if they don't, I will," I've been able to break free from the fear-driven thinking that once held me back.

- **Taking Action Despite Fear:** Building courage and taking action despite fear has been a challenging experience for me. I've learned that fear often almost dissolves when I face it head-on. By consistently pushing myself out of my comfort zone, I've discovered that I'm capable of achieving far more than I ever thought possible. This newfound confidence has enabled me to break through my limitations and make significant progress toward my goals.

- **Surrounding Myself with Supportive People**: In my journey to overcome fear, seeking guidance and encouragement from people and books that I consider to be mentors and peers has been one of the most invaluable things in my life. Their wisdom and experiences have provided me with new perspectives and helped me develop practical strategies to tackle my fears. Their encouragement and belief in my abilities have motivated me to keep moving forward even in the face of real tough times. This support network has been a crucial source of inspiration and accountability, reminding me that I'm not alone in my struggles and that, together, we can overcome any challenge.

- **Creative Expression through Writing:** Writing has been a powerful tool for me in confronting and managing my fears. Putting my thoughts and emotions onto paper has allowed me to gain clarity and understand the root causes of my anxiety. Through storytelling, I've discovered that I can create characters who embody my fears and work through them in a safe, fictional environment. Journaling has also been beneficial, as it enables me to track my progress and identify patterns in my thoughts and behaviours. This process has been instrumental in developing self-awareness and building resilience in the face of fear.

- **Ice-Cold Showers**: Taking ice-cold showers for 45 seconds has been a revealing practice for me. At first, the idea seemed so bloody daunting, fearful shall we say, but as I gradually exposed myself to the cold, I noticed a significant shift in my mindset. The intense sensation of cold water made me more mindful and present in the moment, helping me break free from my fear-inducing thoughts. Over time, this practice has increased my mental toughness and resilience, allowing me to face challenges with a newfound sense of confidence. The cold exposure also triggers the release of endorphins, which has helped me manage stress and anxiety more effectively.

These strategies have been instrumental in my journey to overcome fear, and I hope they can inspire and support you on your own path to facing and conquering your fears.

My Grandad's Funeral

As I stood at my grandad's funeral, I struggled to believe he was gone. He was such an integral part of our family, and it was hard to imagine a world without him. Soon, I realised I had an important responsibility as his eldest grandchild – giving a speech in his honour, a role he had always embraced.

Preparing my notes, I couldn't help but recall being called a loser, feeling fear and anxiety creeping up on me. My Grandad, a barrister and university lecturer, was admired for his eloquence and poise. I felt the pressure of living up to his legacy, terrified of embarrassing myself in front of everyone.

The day of the service arrived, and as I began to walk up to the stand, nerves took over. My hands were shaking, my voice trembling, sweat beading on my forehead. But as I talked about my Grandad's life, legacy, and what he meant to me, something extraordinary happened. I felt his spirit guiding me, giving me the words to say.

As a confident person who had spent his life speaking in front of classes, juries, and audiences, my Grandad had clearly left his mark on me. Fear and anxiety dissipated, and I spoke with newfound confidence and grace. It was as if my Grandad was speaking through me, and I knew I was making him proud.

Reflecting on that day, I realise it was one of the defining moments of my life. It taught me that even in the face of fear and self-doubt, we have the power to endure and overcome. It showed me that sometimes, the greatest source of strength, courage and power can come from those we've loved and lost.

If you find yourself struggling with fear, remember my Grandad's story. Know that even in the darkest moments, there is always a way to find the light. And with the right mindset and courage, you can conquer anything life throws your way.

TASK

We all experience fear from time to time – fear of failure, fear of rejection, or fear of the unknown. While fear can be a natural and healthy emotion, it can also be paralysing, holding us back from living our best lives. That's why it's crucial to develop tools and a mindset to overcome our fears and move forward with confidence.

In this task, we'll explore practical steps you can take to identify and conquer your fears. From checking facts over fiction to visualising success, these exercises will help you build resilience and inner strength to handle life's challenges. So, grab a pen and paper, and let's embark on the path toward fearlessness and personal growth.

Step #1: Identifying Your Fears

- Set aside some quiet time for self-reflection. This will help you focus on your thoughts and emotions without distractions.
- Create a fear inventory by listing all the fears you can think of, no matter how big or small they may seem. Categorise them into different areas of your life such as relationships, career, and personal growth.
- For each fear, identify the underlying thoughts, feelings, and beliefs associated with it. This will help you better understand the root cause of your fears.
- Rank your fears based on their impact on your life and well-being. This will help you prioritise which fears to address first.

Step #2: Fact or Fiction?

- For each fear, examine the thoughts and beliefs you have about it. Ask yourself if they are based on facts or assumptions. Are they helping or hindering you?
- Research and gather factual information related to your fears. This can help you make more informed decisions and challenge any false beliefs or assumptions.
- Challenge negative or limiting beliefs by replacing them with more realistic and empowering thoughts. This can help shift your perspective and reduce the power your fears hold over you.

Step #3: Visualise Success

- Set aside time each day to visualise yourself overcoming your fears and achieving your desired outcomes. Make this a regular practice, ideally at the same time and in the same place each day.
- Use all your senses to create a vivid mental image of your success. Imagine how you will feel, what you will see, and what you will hear when you have overcome your fear.
- Incorporate positive affirmations and self-talk into your visualisation practice. Repeat phrases such as "I am a winner" or "I am strong" to reinforce your belief in your ability to overcome your fears.

Step #4: Take Small Steps

- Break down your fear into smaller, more manageable steps. This can help make the process of overcoming your fear feel less overwhelming.

- Create an action plan for each fear, with specific tasks and deadlines for completion. This will help you stay organised and accountable throughout the process.
- Celebrate your progress as you complete each step. This can help maintain motivation and build confidence in your ability to overcome your fears.

Step #5: Practice Mindfulness

- Incorporate mindfulness meditation into your daily routine. Start with just a few minutes per day and gradually increase the duration as you become more comfortable with the practice.
- Focus on your breath during meditation, and allow thoughts and feelings to come and go without judgment. This can help you develop greater awareness and acceptance of your fears.
- Use mindfulness techniques throughout your day, such as mindful breathing or body scans, to help stay present and grounded in the moment.

Step #6: Celebrate Your Successes

- Keep track of your progress in a journal or use a tracking app to monitor your achievements. This can help you stay motivated and focused on your goals.
- Share your successes with supportive friends, family members, or a therapist. This can help you build a strong support network and gain valuable feedback and encouragement.
- Reflect on your journey and the lessons you have learned along the way. This can help you continue to grow and develop resilience in the face of future challenges.

Chapter 4

BUILDING RESILIENCE

I still remember the first-time life really knocked me down to my knees, leaving me feeling bruised and defeated. It was a time in my life when members of my family were giving me grocery shopping and my mum had to lend me money for my rent because of my naïve habits and choices. In that moment I borrowed that money from my mum as a fully grown adult, I had a choice: to stay down or get up. I chose to rise, and an inner strength allowed me to rebuild my life and ultimately thrive. My mind began building resilience.

Developing a resilient mind at any point in life can be challenging but extremely beneficial in the long run. Resilience helps you cope with stressful situations and prepares you for life's challenges. We are never promised a problem-free life – those picture-perfect moments on social media only show the highlights.

Building resilience can transform your life by equipping you with the ability to adapt and overcome adversity. This leads to improved mental health, reduced stress, and increased confidence. By training your mind to be resilient, you'll see the positive in challenging situations and become a stronger, more confident individual.

Developing resilience requires dedication and commitment. It doesn't happen overnight; it's a lifelong journey. The rewards, however, are well worth the effort. Resilience allows you to view obstacles as opportunities for growth, fostering a sense of empowerment and control over your life. As the saying goes, "No pain, no gain." Embracing challenges and persevering unlocks your full potential and creates a more fulfilling life. With resilience, you'll not only weather any storm but emerge stronger and wiser on the other side.

FOUR ESSENTIAL STEPS TO BECOMING A RESILIENT PERSON

- Changing your outlook
- Challenging your beliefs
- Accepting failure
- Practicing gratitude

Changing your outlook

Let's start with number 1. A negative outlook might sound like this:

- "Nothing ever goes right for me."
- "I can't do anything right."
- "I'm never going to be successful at that."
- "Why bother trying? It's not going to make a difference."
- "I'm just not good enough."
- "It's their fault it is like this."

I've certainly had these thoughts at various points in my life, and they never helped. They only piled on more stress and kept me in a low mood. It's crucial to change a negative outlook because what we focus on creates more of the same in our lives. If you focus on what's wrong or could go wrong, you'll always find more wrong things in your life. It's a natural law.

I used to feel like I wasn't good enough when things didn't go my way. I'd dwell on the negatives, feeling like a victim of circumstance. But that mentality wasn't serving me well and certainly wasn't building resilience. So, I decided to change my thought process and focus on the positives. And you know what? It worked. Instead of feeling defeated, I started feeling grateful for the blessings in my life. Even in unfavourable situations, I found things to be thankful for.

Maybe you have a supportive family, loyal friends, good health, a stable job, or a roof over your head. Or maybe it's as simple as waking up to another day or enjoying a cup of coffee. By focusing on these blessings, you can shift your perspective and find hope and joy, even in difficult times.

But developing appreciation isn't just about feeling good in the moment. It's also about building resilience for the long haul. By recognising the good in your life, you'll be better equipped to handle adversity when it comes your way. You'll have a strong foundation to fall back on, and you'll be able to approach challenges with a more positive and proactive attitude.

So, if you want to build resilience and start feeling more positive about your life, start appreciating what you have in your life experience today. Make a list of the blessings in your life, and take time every day to reflect on them. By doing so, you'll be well on your way to a stronger, more resilient mindset.

As I navigated life's challenges, I encountered obstacles that tested my strength and resilience. At times, it felt like the world was against me, and there was no way out. But it was during these moments that I realised I had the power to change my outlook and build my resilience.

The first step in changing your outlook is acknowledging that difficult situations are an inevitable part of life. They don't define you as a person, nor do they reflect your worth or abilities. When you begin to see adversity as an opportunity for growth and learning, you open yourself up to a whole new world of possibilities.

It's also important to reflect on your strengths and focus on them during challenging times. Your strengths represent your unique qualities and abilities that can help you overcome any challenge that comes your way. By identifying and nurturing your strengths, you build a solid foundation of resilience that can carry you through even the toughest times.

Practicing self-care, which we'll discuss further in upcoming chapters, is another crucial step in building resilience. This involves taking care of your physical, emotional, and mental health, and doing things that bring you joy and satisfaction. Seeking support from loved ones during difficult times is also important, as they can provide a listening ear or practical advice that can help you navigate challenging situations with greater ease.

Remember that every challenge you face is an opportunity to grow and learn. By approaching difficult situations with a positive outlook, you can emerge from them stronger and more capable than before. It is through adversity that we discover our true strength and resilience, and by facing it head-on, we can become the best versions of ourselves.

I truly believe that what you place your focus on will always expand and grow. So, during challenging times, your outlook should always try to be positive. By focusing on the good, you can create more opportunities and open more doors for yourself, realising that you can do it. Maintaining a high vibration and positive attitude will help you stay motivated and energised, even when faced with difficult tasks.

Building a strong, healthy body is a worthy goal that requires hard work and dedication. But setbacks can happen, and negative self-talk can be a real difficulty to overcome. That's exactly what happened to me when I suffered a series of dislocated shoulders during my exercise routine. Negative thoughts flooded my mind, and it was difficult to find the motivation to continue.

It's important to understand that negative self-talk can hold us back during difficult times, whether we're dealing with an injury, loss, or any other challenging circumstance. It can drag us down, sap our confidence, and leave us feeling helpless and demotivated. That's why it's essential to actively work on replacing negative self-talk with more positive self-talk and healthy coping strategies.

For me, mindfulness was key. I started paying close attention to my thoughts and making a conscious effort to replace negative self-talk with positive affirmations like "You're stronger than you think," "You can overcome this," and "This is just a test of your determination." I also prioritised rest as part of a healthy coping strategy. By taking breaks when needed, I gave myself permission to recharge and reminded myself that I'm only human.

It wasn't easy, but I eventually found the determination and motivation I needed to keep pushing forward. The results have been amazing. I've overcome my difficulties and built a physique I'm really proud of. I have more energy, confidence, and strength than ever before, and I'm grateful to myself for pushing through.

The truth is, developing a positive mindset and healthy coping strategies can make all the difference in building resilience during difficult times. It takes practice, but once you start making an effort to replace negative self-talk with positive self-talk, you'll be amazed at how much more confident and motivated you feel.

The key takeaway here is that with a positive mindset and healthy self-talk, you can cultivate resilience and push through difficulties, no matter how daunting they might seem. So, if you're facing challenges right now, be mindful of your thoughts and make a conscious effort to replace any negative self-talk with a more positive perspective. Remember, you're stronger than you think, and you can overcome anything as long as you have the right mindset.

"God didn't promise us a problem-free life; we are never going to have that. You are never going to experience life and feel like everything is going well all the time. But there has to be something inside of you, even right now today, that decides you're going to win, no matter what." – Nicki Minaj

Challenging your beliefs

What are beliefs? Beliefs are personal convictions or principles that we as humans hold to be true or important. They often guide our behaviour, decision-making, and outlook on life. Challenging beliefs means questioning them and evaluating whether they are accurate, relevant, or helpful in our lives.

Beliefs can be powerful, and at times, they can be so powerful they hold us back from reaching our full potential. We may hold onto beliefs without even realising it, and these beliefs may be deeply ingrained in our psyche. They may be embedded in our values, attitudes, and behaviours. Our beliefs can determine our level of happiness, health, and success.

It is important to understand that beliefs are not absolute truths. They are simply our interpretations of experiences we have had in our lives. As we grow and learn, we may need to adjust our beliefs accordingly. By challenging our beliefs, we can gain a deeper understanding of ourselves and the world around us.

So, how can we challenge our beliefs? The first step is to identify them. Take some time to reflect on your beliefs and try to understand where they came from. Were they instilled in you by your family or culture? Did you form them based on personal experiences? Once you have identified your beliefs, examine them and ask yourself whether they are accurate, relevant, and helpful in your life.

It is also important to be open-minded and listen to others' viewpoints. This will give you a broader perspective and enable you to see things from different angles. You may also find that some of your beliefs are limiting you and preventing you from achieving your goals. By challenging and changing these beliefs, you can unlock your full potential and lead a more fulfilling life.

Another way to challenge your beliefs is by facing your fears. Fear is often rooted in limiting beliefs and can prevent us from taking risks and trying new things. By facing your fears and taking action, you can prove to yourself that your limiting beliefs are not true. This will give you a sense of empowerment and boost your confidence.

In summary, beliefs are a powerful driving force in our lives, but they are not set in stone. By challenging our beliefs and being open-minded, we can gain a deeper understanding of ourselves and others. We can also unlock our full potential and lead a more fulfilling life. So, take some time to reflect on your beliefs, examine them, and be open to new perspectives. The rewards will be worth it.

Here are my top 5 reasons why challenging your beliefs is crucial for your self-development:

- **Helps you identify and correct irrational beliefs:** Sometimes, we hold onto beliefs that are not true and do not serve us well. By challenging our beliefs, we can identify which ones are rational and which ones are not. This allows us to correct our thinking and replace irrational or negative beliefs with more positive and helpful ones, opening up phenomenal opportunities.

- **Encourages flexibility:** Life is full of unexpected events, and having the ability to adapt to new situations and perspectives is key to developing resilience. Challenging our beliefs can help us become more open-minded and flexible in our thinking, allowing us to adjust to new situations in a more constructive and adaptive way. If you encounter something you don't necessarily like or is not favourable, try to see it from a different perspective, knowing in your heart that what is meant for you will never pass you by.

- **Builds confidence and self-efficacy:** Challenging our beliefs and successfully replacing them with more helpful ones can also build confidence and a sense of self-efficacy. When we are able to reframe our thinking and overcome challenges, we feel more capable and empowered to handle future obstacles.

- **Strengthens empathy and understanding:** Engaging with different perspectives of our beliefs helps us appreciate the diversity of human experiences. This can enhance our ability to empathise and form deeper connections with others.

- **Avoids stagnation:** Refusing to acknowledge that our beliefs can change, or even questioning them, can leave us in a place where we are stuck or close-minded. Challenging our beliefs creates an opportunity to increase our intellectual curiosity and cultivates a willingness to learn and grow.

Dave's Story: Challenging His Beliefs for a Better Life

Dave had always struggled with apprehension and negative self-talk. He felt stuck in a cycle of self-doubt and fear that held him back from pursuing his real dreams. But then, he stumbled upon the idea of challenging his beliefs.

At first, Dave was hesitant. He had been told from a young age that his beliefs were who he was and that questioning them was unthinkable. But something inside him told him that it was time to try something new and expand his horizons.

He began by examining his beliefs about his abilities. He had always believed that he was not smart enough, not good enough, and not skilled enough to achieve his biggest aspirations. But as he examined these beliefs, he realised that they were not based on facts but simply his own negative self-talk.

We all have that voice in our head, the nagging voice that convinces us to play it safe and stay within our comfort zone. This negative voice can be incredibly convincing. It's the same voice that tells us we're not good enough, that we'll never succeed, and that we shouldn't challenge our beliefs. But here's the thing that Dave discovered: that voice is not actually us. It's the result of years of conditioning, the beliefs we've internalised from our environment, upbringing, and past experiences. We wouldn't choose to think negatively about ourselves – yet that voice persists. However, when we acknowledge that this voice is not our own and actively work to challenge these beliefs, we build resilience and gain greater control over our thoughts and actions.

For Dave, that voice had been holding him back for too long. He was a talented painter and decorator but was convinced that he couldn't bring himself to create a side hustle with his passion and talent for photography.

Dave's negative self-talk had become a barrier to his success, preventing him from earning more and expanding his skill set. But deep down, he knew that he had the potential to excel as a photographer if he just believed in himself and challenged his self-limiting beliefs.

He set out to prove the voice wrong by looking for evidence to the contrary. He researched business, photography, and lighting courses and found a combined course that would help him develop his skills and create his side hustle. But as the day of the class drew near, his old doubts crept back in. Could he really do this? Was he good enough? What if nothing came of it?

Dave knew he had to overcome his negative self-talk and take a leap of faith. He would never know what he was capable of if he didn't try. So, he signed up for the class and showed up with an open mind.

To his surprise, Dave found that not only did he learn quickly, but he actually enjoyed the class more than he had expected and made some new friends with valuable insights and ideas. He had challenged his belief that he was not capable of taking his skills to the next level and discovered that the voice had been wrong all along. Dave had not only built his skills to become a fantastic and in-demand photographer, but he had also built resilience by challenging his beliefs and negative self-talk.

As Dave continued to challenge his other beliefs, he found that his apprehension began to lessen. He realised that many of his fears were based on irrational beliefs that he had held onto for too long. In replacing these beliefs with more rational and positive ones, he began to feel more confident in himself and his abilities.

But perhaps the most unexpected benefit of challenging his beliefs was that it helped him become more empathetic toward others. By exploring different perspectives and questioning his own assumptions, he developed a deeper understanding of the diversity of human experience. This newfound understanding made it easier for him to connect with others and treat them with more compassion and kindness.

Dave's story of challenging his beliefs is an excellent example of building resilience. Resilience is the ability to adapt and bounce back from adversity, and it's crucial for our personal growth and development. By challenging his beliefs, Dave was able to overcome his fears and self-doubt, and develop a more positive outlook on life. This positive outlook has helped him face life's challenges with a greater sense of optimism and strength.

Today, Dave is living a life that he loves. He is pursuing his dreams and achieving new goals with a newfound sense of confidence and self-efficacy. Recently, he was even invited to the Amazon rainforest to photograph some of the most beautiful landscapes and animal species in the world. Dave credits his willingness to challenge his beliefs with helping him break free from the negative thought patterns that had held him back for so long.

Through his journey, Dave has learned that challenging our beliefs is not only crucial for personal development but can also lead to a more fulfilling and satisfying life. It takes courage to examine our beliefs, but the rewards are truly phenomenal. Dave's newfound confidence and self-efficacy have allowed him to pursue his dreams and achieve his goals with renewed passion and purpose, no longer holding himself back.

In conclusion, challenging our beliefs helps us build resilience by allowing us to develop a more positive and flexible perspective, greater self-awareness, and a stronger sense of confidence in our ability to navigate the challenging situations and surprising experiences that life offers. By embracing the courage to question our beliefs and assumptions, we can open ourselves up to a world of growth, resilience, and opportunities beyond our wildest dreams.

LEARNING TO ACCEPT FAILURE

Learning to accept failure is our next pillar in building resilience. Failure is never easy to experience, but one of my favourite stories of someone who experienced

failure and refused to allow it to affect their spirit—
ultimately noticing that failure led them to huge
success—is Michael Jordan.

During high school, Michael Jordan tried out for the
varsity basketball team but wasn't able to make the
team. Although this was a blow to Michael, he refused to
give up. He practiced even harder and joined the junior
varsity team. Through sheer determination, he ultimately
made the varsity team. His unwavering work ethic,
ambition, and discipline helped him become one of the
best basketball players of all time.

Michael Jordan's story is a brilliant example of how
failure is simply a stage in the process toward success.
By putting in the hard work and effort, learning from his
mistakes, and maintaining a positive attitude, he was
able to persist and become one of the most well-known
and celebrated athletes in the world. He is still talked
about now, over 20 years after his retirement.

Jordan knew in his heart what he wanted to do and
recognised that success is not based on the number of
failures you experience, but rather how you respond to
those failures. This quote by Jordan sums up why we
should keep going through our challenges, regardless of
how many come along:

*"I have missed more than 9,000 shots in my career. I
have lost almost 300 games. On 26 occasions, I have
been entrusted to take the game-winning shot, and I
missed. I have failed over and over and over again in
my life. And that is why I succeed."*

Learning to acknowledge and accept failure is an
essential part of building resilience throughout life.
Despite our best efforts, failure is inevitable - whether it's
a small setback or a significant obstacle. It can be

disheartening and zap the motivation out of anyone. However, accepting failure can be a powerful tool for developing mental toughness and resilience, ultimately leading to success through continuous learning and determined effort.

One of the biggest roadblocks to progress is the fear of failure. Many people avoid taking risks that could lead to a negative outcome or view it as a personal fault. This often presents a more significant challenge than the failure itself, hindering growth and development. Accepting failure teaches us to let go of the fear of the unknown and embrace challenges instead of avoiding them. With each failure, we gain experience and learn valuable lessons that help us improve for next time.

Max's Story: Embracing Failure for Success

Let me share the story of Maximilian, or Max for short. Max had always dreamed of starting his own business but was held back by the fear of failure. He was convinced that if he tried and failed, it would be the end of the world. So, he never even attempted to pursue his dreams.

Years went by, and Max watched those around him achieve high success – starting their own businesses, becoming CEOs, and making a name for themselves in the world of entrepreneurship. But Max remained stuck in his fear, unable to try, even though he knew deep down that he was capable of achieving greatness.

One day, Max stumbled upon a self-help book titled "You are the chosen one." It was the catalyst he needed to finally act. The book taught Max that failure was a natural part of life's journey, and that successful people don't achieve success by simply never failing. They achieve success by failing, learning from their mistakes, and persevering in the face of adversity.

Initially skeptical, Max began to feel a sense of hope as he read the book. He realised that he could self-develop, and that failure wasn't something to be feared - it was something to be embraced. Slowly but surely, Max started taking action, networking with other entrepreneurs, attending start-up events, and learning about successful business practices.

Max met with several setbacks in his journey. His first business idea failed, and he faced rejection from investors and customers alike. But instead of giving up, Max picked himself back up and tried again. He spent time reflecting on his past mistakes and what he could do differently in the future. He learned to view his failures as opportunities to grow and improve, rather than as reasons to give up.

As he grew more resilient, Max's confidence grew as well. He started to see his past failures as stepping stones on the path to success. Eventually, Max launched his second business, more prepared, focused, and determined than ever before. And to his surprise, his business began to thrive.

As he watched his business grow and flourish, Max realised that his fear of failure had been holding him back all along. He had been so afraid of failing that he never even gave himself the chance to succeed.

Learning to accept failure is an important part of building resilience throughout life. It helps us to reframe adversity and build the confidence to tackle new challenges. Through experience, reflection, and learning, we can use failure as a tool to make better-informed decisions and improve our chances of success in the future.

As Tony Robbins once said, "As scary as failure can be, it is often our greatest friend in disguise, for it is through our mistakes that we learn, grow, and ultimately thrive." Embracing failure allows us to build resilience and create a pathway to success.

Gratitude: A Powerful Tool for Resilience

As we've discussed, building resilience is crucial for personal development. Life can throw various obstacles our way, and resilience helps us bounce back and keep going. One effective way to build resilience, and my personal favourite due to its simplicity, is through the practice of gratitude.

Gratitude transforms your life by focusing on the positive aspects rather than the negative ones. It reminds us of the good things we have, instead of dwelling on what we lack. Incorporating gratitude into your daily life can help develop unshakable inner strength, allowing you to overcome challenges with ease.

Oprah Winfrey exemplifies the power of gratitude. Despite facing numerous obstacles, she remained positive and resilient, crediting gratitude for helping her stay focused and spirited. In her book "What I Know for Sure," Oprah shares her experience overcoming depression by focusing on things she was grateful for, like her friends, family, health, and successful TV career. This shift in perspective enabled her to see that, despite her struggles, she still had a lot to be grateful for.

Oprah continues to practice gratitude, making it a daily habit to write down five things she's grateful for and encouraging others to do the same. To build resilience and transform your life, start incorporating gratitude into your routine. Take a few moments each day to reflect on the things you're grateful for, whether it's your health, friends and family, or something small like a delicious cup of coffee or significant like a loving relationship. With practice, you'll see the world in a new light, focusing on the positive and developing inner strength to overcome any obstacle.

As Wayne Dyer said, "Those who are loving, live in a loving world, those who are hostile, live in a hostile world, same world." Gratitude is a powerful tool that can help you build resilience and overcome tough challenges. By practicing gratitude daily, you can shift your focus from what you lack to what you have, and develop an unshakable inner strength to bounce back from any setback. So, start practicing gratitude today and watch your life transform before your very eyes.

Building Resilience Through Gratitude

Now that we know gratitude is key to building resilience, let's explore simple yet effective techniques to cultivate it.

Firstly, keeping a gratitude journal can be incredibly beneficial. Make it a daily ritual to write down five things you're grateful for, no matter how big or small. This helps shift your focus away from the negative and cultivates an attitude of gratitude in your daily life.

Now that we've discussed the importance of gratitude journaling, let's explore additional ways to build resilience through gratitude.

One powerful method is to practice mindfulness. By being present in the moment without judgment, we can find joy in the small things we typically overlook. Immersing yourself in each moment, like taking a deep breath or savouring your morning coffee, shows you how beautiful even the simplest aspects of life can be. Mindfulness reduces stress and anxiety, which can be detrimental to resilience, and enables us to cope better with challenges.

Another crucial aspect is having a sense of purpose. When we feel our life has meaning and we are contributing to something bigger than ourselves, it contributes positively to forming a more grateful mindset, enabling you to tackle adversity more effectively.

Additionally, let's not forget the importance of self-care in building resilience through gratitude. The path to self-development is filled with hurdles, and taking care of ourselves is vital in navigating those challenges. Self-care can take on many forms and varies from person to person. By prioritising our emotional, physical, and spiritual health, we become better equipped to handle life's unexpected twists and turns with grace and gratitude. We will delve further into the vital role of self-care in self-development in an upcoming chapter, so stay tuned for more insights and inspiration.

Incorporating these practices into your daily routine will help you build resilience through gratitude, enabling you to thrive no matter what challenges come your way. Remember, every day offers an opportunity to appreciate the positive things in your life. Take advantage of this and see the world with fresh eyes.

TASK

―――――――――――――

Are you now ready to go on your journey to become an unstoppable force in the face of adversity? Let's dive in and explore six empowering steps to strengthen your resilience. You may not realise it, but your mindset holds the key to conquering any obstacle that comes your way. This task will help you reflect on your thoughts and beliefs, challenging any negative patterns that may be holding you back. It's time to embrace failure as a powerful learning opportunity, cultivate gratitude, nurture your relationships, and embrace change. Integrating these steps into your daily life will cultivate unwavering resilience, making you unstoppable. So, let's begin your journey to becoming a resilient champion in life!

Step #1: Self-reflection

Start by setting aside time each day for the next 7 days to reflect on your thoughts and beliefs. Writing them down is crucial as it helps identify any negative or limiting beliefs you've been holding onto. Once identified, you can begin challenging these beliefs using the methods outlined in this chapter. Acknowledge your feelings, strengths, and limitations, and work on them to learn and grow.

Step #2: Challenging negative beliefs

The next step is to challenge these negative beliefs by asking yourself tough questions. Ask yourself if they are really true. Have there been times when you've been successful despite feeling inadequate or unsure? Are there other ways to view the situation more positively or empowering? By doing this, you'll break down limiting beliefs and start seeing things in a more positive light.

Step #3: Accept failure as an opportunity

Accepting failure is crucial to building resilience. Recognise that every failure provides an opportunity to learn and grow. Make a list of things you've tried in the past that didn't work out. Instead of seeing them as failures, view them as valuable learning experiences that allowed you to grow and develop new skills. Write down the lessons learned from each experience and reflect on how they've contributed to your personal growth.

Step #4: Cultivate gratitude

Gratitude shifts our focus from negativity to positivity. Practice gratitude daily to develop an optimistic outlook. Take a few minutes each day to reflect on things in your life you're thankful for. This can include people in your life, opportunities you've had, or moments of joy you've experienced. Write down 3 things you're grateful for every day before bed and read them upon waking up. Make this a habit, and your resilience to any challenge will only grow stronger.

Step #5: Nurture your relationships

Strong relationships are essential for building resilience. They provide emotional support and help maintain perspective during difficult situations. Nurture your relationships by spending time with supportive people who uplift you. Look for opportunities to connect with others, express gratitude for those around you, and always be willing to lend a listening ear.

Step #6: Welcome change

Change is an unavoidable part of life. Building resilience means learning to embrace change and adapt to it. Since change is the only constant in life, it's essential to develop the ability to adjust to new situations quickly. Challenge yourself by stepping out of your comfort zone, and practice being comfortable with uncertainty, knowing that it will only help you grow stronger.

Building resilience is not just a good idea—it's a vital skill everyone should develop. Life is unpredictable, and challenges are inevitable. Resilient individuals have the ability to bounce back from setbacks, adapt to change, and face challenges with confidence and courage. They cultivate flexibility, maintain a growth mindset, and develop coping skills. Although building resilience takes practice and patience, every effort towards developing this skill is worthwhile. It is an integral part of the self-development journey and can help you achieve your goals, live an authentic life, and become your best self.

From my personal experience, I believe everyone has the potential to achieve great things. However, to do so, you must face and overcome obstacles. You have the power to conquer challenges and turn your dreams into reality. Building resilience is one of the essential tools you need to make that happen. This journey requires patience, perseverance, and practice, but it's a journey worth taking.

So, keep building your resistance, stay powerful, and embrace the journey with positivity, purpose, and inner strength. Onwards and upwards!

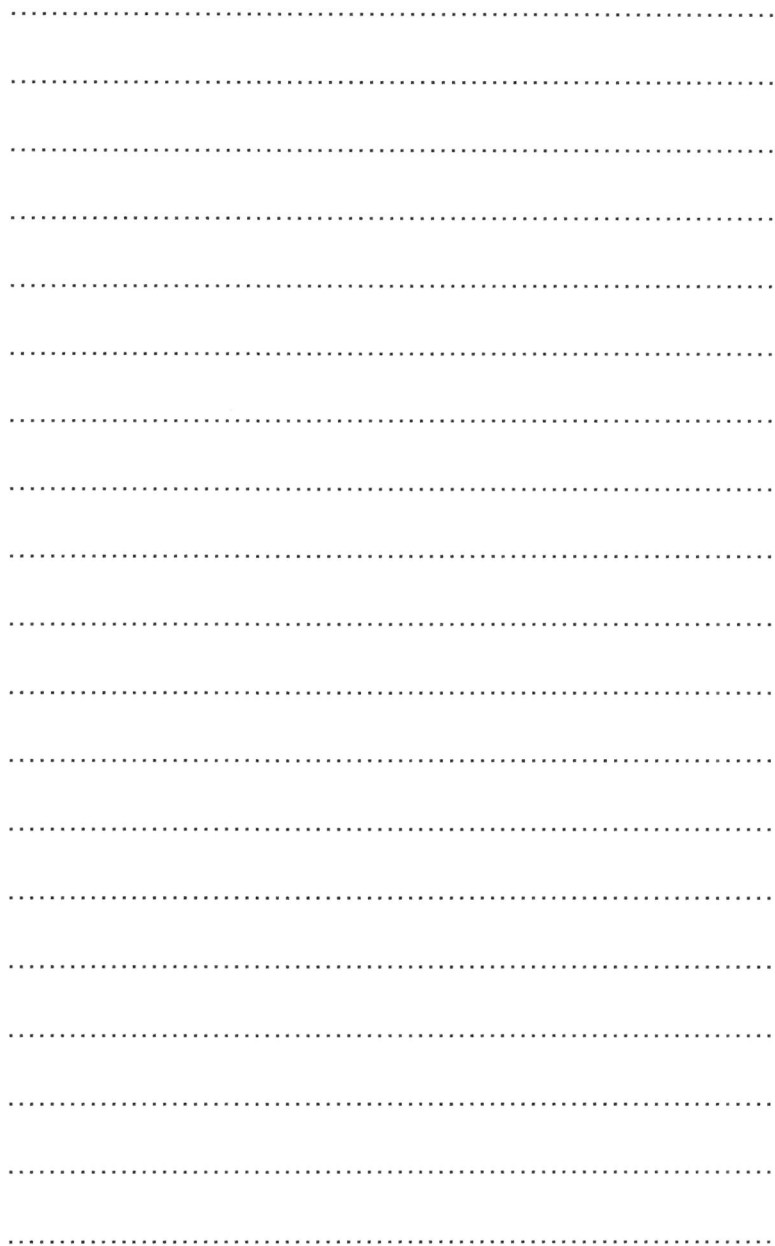

....

....

....

....

....

....

....

"It ain't about how hard you hit. It's about how hard you can get hit and keep moving forward. How much you can take and keep moving forward. That's how winning is done. - Rocky Balboa
MGM Studios

Chapter 5

SETTING AND ACHIEVING YOUR GOALS

When I quit smoking, I had a desire to become a runner—but the thought of covering even a short distance without losing my breath seemed like an impossible dream. Despite my doubts, I decided to make it my goal. I wanted to prove to myself that I could overcome the obstacles and transform my life for the better. The journey was far from easy, with moments when my lungs burned and my legs ached, but my determination never wavered. Gradually, my strength and endurance grew. By setting a clear goal, staying committed, and believing in myself, I turned my dream into reality.

Have you ever heard someone say,

"What's the point of setting goals? I'll never achieve them anyway?"

If that's your attitude towards goal setting, you're creating a self-fulfilling prophecy. Your mindset and attitude play a crucial role in achieving your goals. As Henry Ford once said,

"He who thinks he can, and he who thinks he can't, are both right."

Adopting a positive and growth-oriented mindset when setting goals is crucial. Believe in yourself, have faith in your ideas, and trust that you're capable of achieving whatever you set your mind to. This mindset will help you stay focused, motivated, and resilient, even when the going gets tough.

Goals should be personal and meaningful to you, reflecting your unique desires and aspirations. They should inspire you to keep pushing forward. Goals give us direction and help us stay on track, even when the journey towards them is challenging and unpredictable.

Desires are the starting point for any goal-setting process. They provide the motivation and direction for us to work towards specific goals and create action plans. When you desire something strongly enough, you begin to actively pursue ways to achieve it, leading to the creation of specific goals.

Having a clear sense of desire can help you stay interested and dedicated to your goals, even during setbacks and challenges. Desires serve as the driving force behind goal formation, providing the necessary direction, motivation, and focus for us to make our aspirations and dreams a reality.

Understanding Our Desires

Have you ever pondered what truly motivates you in life? Are you aware of your deepest desires? Often, we go through life without understanding ourselves and what we want out of it. However, having a clear vision of our desires is crucial to achieve the success and fulfilment we crave.

Recently, I listened to one of my favourite speakers, Mel Robbins, discussing the power of jealousy. Surprisingly, jealousy can be a helpful emotion when used positively. It serves as a signpost to identify what we want in life. Jealousy can ignite our motivation and inspire us to take action towards achieving our goals.

Traditionally, jealousy has been seen as a daunting emotion rooted in fear. But life coach extraordinaire, Mel Robbins, argues that jealousy is actually a form of blocked fear. This means it can be a valuable tool for self-understanding. For example, if someone close to us achieves a goal we have no interest in, we feel happy for them but not envious. However, if their achievement aligns with our deep-seated desires, it can trigger jealousy.

Jealousy can help us understand our life's meaning and purpose by revealing our desires' significance. When used wisely and processing our feelings in a healthy way, it motivates us to strive for the things we want in life. Jealousy provides clarity on the goals we should set for ourselves.

We all desire things in life that bring us pleasure and happiness, but we need to ensure that our goals align with our personal values. When our goals are consistent with our values, we experience a sense of purpose and fulfilment that cannot be found in material success alone.

Take the time to discover your desires and ensure your goals align with them. Use jealousy as a tool to understand your deepest desires and motivations. Once you have clarity, set your goals and take action towards achieving them. Remember, your desires are unique to you, and only you can create the life you truly want.

Our Values: The Compass Guiding Our Journey

Life is a journey filled with twists and turns, and it's crucial to have a guiding compass that directs our decisions and actions. Setting and achieving goals serves as that compass, leading us towards our desired destination. To set meaningful goals, we need clarity about our personal values—the core principles that shape our lives.

Reflecting on my values, I've come to realise that they're deeply intertwined with my experiences and aspirations. At the core of my being lies integrity, the unwavering backbone of my moral compass. It's what drives me to uphold high standards in every facet of life, always striving to be the best version of myself.

My insatiable curiosity fuels my commitment to personal growth. Each experience becomes an opportunity to learn and evolve, fostering a continuous journey of self-improvement. And when the going gets tough, it's perseverance that carries me through. This unstoppable force pushes me to overcome obstacles and persevere in the face of adversity.

Trust is paramount in any relationship, which is why accountability holds such significance for me. Taking responsibility for my actions and staying true to my commitments isn't just a value I hold dear—it's a testament to who I am.

I've always believed in the power of collaboration and the joy that comes from uplifting others. Helping my friends achieve their goals is a value close to my heart, a testament to my conviction that we're stronger together.

Perhaps what truly sets me apart is my unwavering commitment to getting things done. The thrill of accomplishing tasks—no matter how daunting they seem—energises me in a way nothing else can. My partner affectionately calls me "Sargent Major" due to my determination and the way I tackle challenges head-on. This dogged persistence enables me to stay focused and conquer goals that initially appear impossible.

Underpinning it all is honour, the foundation upon which my integrity and steadfastness are built. It's the glue that binds my values together, guiding my actions and reminding me of the man I strive to be each day.

As you travel through your self-development journey, it's crucial to identify your own personal values. These values act as your guiding light, throw a light on your beliefs and actions. Reflect on moments when you felt truly satisfied or fulfilled—these instances can help pinpoint your core values. Understanding how they align with your beliefs empowers you to live authentically.

Aligning your goals with your values ensures you remain motivated and inspired throughout your journey. For instance, if creativity is one of your core values, pursuing a blog or writing a book can be deeply fulfilling. If making a difference drives you, a career in the non-profit sector could amplify your impact and resonate with your values.

While aligning goals with values is essential, taking action to bring them to fruition is equally important. Accomplishing goals can bring emotional benefits like pride and joy. However, the process of working towards these goals helps you build resilience, develop new skills, and overcome challenges.

Break your goals down into manageable steps, making progress more achievable. Celebrating small victories along the way can sustain your momentum. Be flexible and adapt your plans if needed, as unforeseen obstacles may arise.

In conclusion, understanding your personal values is a vital step in setting and achieving meaningful goals. Your values act as a compass, guiding you towards a fulfilling and purposeful life. By aligning your goals with your values and taking actionable steps to achieve them, you can harness the power of your inner compass and move closer to your desired destination. Remember, as Tony Robbins said, "Progress equals happiness." Act in accordance with your values and they will guide you on your journey to personal growth and success.

The Emotional Significance of Goal Setting and Achievement

Setting and achieving goals is crucial for our emotional wellbeing, and it can have a profound impact on every aspect of our lives and I'll explain why. In this part of the chapter, we'll delve deeper into why setting goals is so important for our emotional wellbeing and offer practical ways to achieve them.

One significant advantage of setting and achieving goals is the positive impact it has on our self-confidence and self-esteem. By setting a goal that pushes us beyond our current capabilities, we demonstrate our belief in our potential for growth. This ambition, which I like to call "put a cap on it," inspires us to reach new heights and accomplish something meaningful we've never done before. When we achieve that goal, we prove to ourselves that we are capable, competent, and worthy of success, leading to greater happiness and satisfaction. This newfound confidence can empower us to tackle even greater challenges and grow in all aspects of our lives.

Another game-changing advantage of setting and achieving goals is the much-needed clarity it brings to our lives. Imagine navigating life with a clear purpose – like a neon light flashing 'Your dreams this way'. When you know what you're striving for, your actions and decisions naturally align with your long-term goals. This alignment creates a sense of order amidst life's chaos, helping you bid farewell to unnecessary stress and anxiety. Ultimately, you'll gain an empowering sense of control over your life's trajectory.

But it doesn't stop there! Achieving our goals awakens a profound sense of purpose and meaning within us. The journey towards your aspirations fuels a fire in your heart, creating a reason to leap out of bed each morning with passion and enthusiasm. Working towards something that truly matters to you not only boosts your engagement in the world around you but also cultivates an enriching sense of fulfilment that amplifies your overall life satisfaction. So, embrace the transformative power of setting and conquering goals – it'll change your life for the better!

It's no secret that we humans crave connection and to thrive in communities. We flourish when we share experiences, celebrate triumphs, and tackle challenges together. Want to know one powerful way to turbocharge your relationships? Set and conquer goals side by side!

Picture this: my partner and I had been dreaming of a Bali getaway for years. Finally, we decided enough was enough – it was time to make it happen! We set a goal to plan and embark on our dream trip within 12 months. Since then, our relationship has soared to new heights.

Researching flights, scouring travel guides, and scrolling through endless blog posts together became our new norm. We grew as a team, mastering the art of communication and cheering each other on through every little victory. Trust me, nothing beats the feeling of smashing goals with your favourite person by your side!

So, if you want to inject some fresh energy into your relationships, give shared goals a shot. Whether it's starting a business, getting fit, or crossing items off your bucket list, working towards a common purpose can weave an unbreakable bond. And hey, you might even surprise yourselves with the memories and accomplishments you collect along the way! Remember, nurturing your relationships is vital to your emotional well-being, and setting meaningful goals together is one fantastic way to do just that.

The Metamorphosis - Releasing Your Ideal Self

Have you ever wondered how it seems some people turn their dreams into reality overnight? What if I told you, it's not quite like that but there is a secret formula that can help you conquer your wildest aspirations?

Prepare to discover the mysteries of self-image and self-ideal – two powerful forces shaping your destiny. This thrilling journey if you choose to take it, will carry you on a rollercoaster ride of growth, sacrifice, and self-discovery, revealing the untapped potential within you.

Diving into personal growth to your goals, it is a life-altering adventure that will leave you inspired, courageous, and ready to take on the world for all your desire.

What is Self-Image?

Self-image is your mental snapshot – a reflection of how you perceive yourself! It's shaped by your beliefs, values, and experiences, influencing your thoughts, emotions, and actions in life's grand arena. Imagine your self-image as the outfit you put on every day, showcasing your confidence, aspirations, and the unique vibe you bring to the world.

What is Self-Ideal?

Self-ideal is your personal superhero – the version of you that's poised, powerful, and ready to conquer any challenge! This guiding light illuminates the path to your dreams, embodying the qualities, skills, and traits necessary for success. Your self-ideal is the ultimate role model, inspiring you to soar to new heights.

The Transformation: From Self-Image to Self-Ideal

When setting out to achieve goals you never have before, the journey from your current self-image to your self-ideal is a wild ride of growth, self-discovery, and accepting of change. As you boldly step out of your comfort zone, prepare to face exhilarating challenges and heart-wrenching sacrifices. Friends may become distant, your favourite club or bar might lose their charm, you could move away and life as you know it may shift completely. Remember, it's okay to shed a tear or two;

it's a testament to your courage and determination of changing your life for the better.

Unlocking Goal Achievement Through Self-Ideal

Crushing your goals becomes a breeze when you align your actions and mindset with your self-ideal. Picture your self-ideal as a master chef; by sharpening those knife skills and perfecting that secret sauce, you become unstoppable in the kitchen we call life! Through each tear and sacrifice, remind yourself of the profound personal growth you're experiencing. The journey doesn't end once you've tasted sweet success; it's a continuous adventure of refining and redefining your self-ideal as you evolve.

If you accept this transformative journey, tears, sacrifices and all, as you shoot forward toward your dreams, it will be worth it. It's through the dance of self-image and self-ideal that you'll unleash your deepest desires and discover the relentless, unstoppable force that lies within you.

Top 5 Tips for Achieving Your Goals

Now that we understand the significance of setting and achieving goals for our emotional wellbeing, let's create a plan of action to help us accomplish our objectives and reach our full potential. Here are my top 5 tips for turning your dreams into reality:

- **Take Action:** Remember, a goal without action is just a daydream! Kickstart your journey with that all-important first step and keep the ball rolling with consistent follow-through. Even the tiniest actions can create massive ripples, so keep at it!

- **Stay Organised:** Wrangle the chaos with a solid organisation game plan! Plot out your moves, set deadlines, and track your progress using your trusty planner or nifty digital tools. Stay focused and on top of your time management game like a boss.

- **Seek Support:** Friends, family, coaches and books – rally your resources! Don't be shy about asking for help, guidance, or a good ol' fashioned pep talk. Whether it's professional coaching, helpful reads, or a heart-to-heart with a loved one, lean on your support system when the going gets tough.

- **Celebrate Your Achievements:** Give yourself a well-deserved pat on the back as you crush those milestones! Celebrating your hard work and progress will keep that fire burning bright and the motivation flowing. Treat yourself, and remember, you're awesome!

- **Stay Flexible:** Life loves to put a spanner in the works, so stay flexible and adaptable! Welcome the inevitable twists and turns, learn from your experiences, and be open to altering or tweaking your strategies as needed. With patience and a continuous learning attitude, you'll be unstoppable!

My secret tip

Welcome to my spiritual realm of goal setting and achievement. Today, I'll reveal my secret tip that has transformed my life and helped me materialise my heart's desires. In my personal journey, I've discovered the profound power of connecting with my higher self through meditation and gaining clarity on my goals and intentions. This deepened sense of self-awareness allows me to experience the exhilarating emotions of achievement even before reaching my objectives.

Spiritual goal setting urges you to release any resistance, such as negative self-talk or limiting beliefs. To overcome these obstacles, nurture your gratitude for how far you have come, trust your intuition to guide you, and have faith that what's meant for you will never pass you by. Use your your inner strength, face challenges head-on, and persevere with unwavering focus and determination.

Now, for the pièce de résistance – the magic of **writing down your goals!** This simple yet powerful act clarifies your desires and solidifies your commitment. Writing down your goals ensures they align with your spiritual values and beliefs, such as compassion, kindness, honesty, and respect. It also bolsters your faith and confidence in your abilities and the universe's divine support.

From a spiritual perspective, penning your goals is a manifestation ritual. It generates potent energy and focus, helping you shape your dreams into reality. As you write, you communicate your intentions to the cosmos, activating the forces that bring your vision to fruition. This practice not only reminds you of your commitment but also fuels your motivation and maintains your focus on your desired outcome. And here's the proof: all my goals, including you reading this very message, were first inscribed on paper, transforming them into manifestations that have come to light.

Encompassing spiritual goal setting can profoundly enhance your life. By connecting with your higher self, practicing gratitude, trusting your intuition, and staying true to your aspirations, you can materialise your deepest desires and live a life aligned with your authentic self. Remember, you are the architect of your destiny, and the power to create your dreams lies within you. Believe in yourself, write down your goals, and take inspired action to make your visions a reality. With trust, patience, and unwavering faith, you can achieve anything you set your mind to. So, trust the process and allow the universe to work its magic in your favour.

"Writing your goals down is like planting a seed in the garden of your soul. You give it your attention, water it with intention, and watch it grow into its full potential. With every step you take towards your written goals, you align more deeply with your true nature and the infinite intelligence that guides us all." - Esther Hicks

TASK

_____

Congratulations on taking the first step towards achieving your goals! Setting and achieving goals is a crucial part of personal growth and development. While it's important to set goals, it's equally essential to develop determination, focus, and an effective plan to successfully accomplish them.

This step-by-step guide will help you set SMART goals, create a plan of action, track your progress, and celebrate your achievements. Each step builds on the previous one, providing a framework for success in all your endeavours.

In addition to the practical steps, we've included a spiritual element. By connecting with your spiritual self and seeking guidance, you can tap into a higher power to help you achieve your goals and manifest your desired reality.

Remember that fulfilling your goals requires patience, effort, and consistency. With the tools and guidance provided, you'll be well on your way to making your dreams a reality.

Step #1: Set a Clear and Concise Goal

Take some time to reflect on what you want to achieve in your life, whether it be in your personal life, love life, career, or health. Write down one specific goal in a clear and concise sentence that is easily understood. Make it specific enough that a 4-year-old could grasp what it is you want to achieve.

Step #2: Create a SMART Goal

Use the SMART (Specific, Measurable, Achievable, Relevant, Time-bound) method to craft an effective goal:
- Specific: Make sure your goal is well-defined and specific to you by addressing the 5W's – Who, What, When, Where, and Why.
- Measurable: Include a form of quantitative or qualitative measurement to track your progress based on milestones.
- Achievable: Consider the skills, resources, and time you have or can acquire to ensure your goal is attainable.
- Relevant: Align your goal with your long-term plans and personal values, bringing you closer to the life you want.
- Time-bound: Set a specific deadline or completion date to create a sense of urgency and motivate consistent action.

Step #3: Develop an Action Plan

Break down your SMART goal into smaller, manageable steps. Write down all the tasks you need to complete, ticking them off as you progress. This step-by-step approach will help you make steady progress toward your objective.

Step #4: Monitor Your Progress

Track your progress against your SMART goals and deadlines. Regularly reviewing your achievements will give you a sense of momentum and accomplishment. It will also help you determine if you need to readjust your plan or take any corrective action to stay on track.

Step #5: Celebrate Your Success

My favourite step in the goal-setting process is acknowledging and celebrating your success upon achieving your SMART goal. Take a moment to appreciate the effort you put in and revel in the realisation that it was all worth it. This step is also an excellent time to evaluate how well you did and identify areas for improvement in your next goal. Completing this task will provide you with a proven framework for setting and achieving any goal, enhancing your self-awareness and positively impacting all aspects of your life. Remember, you deserve to have everything you want, so keep setting and achieving those goals!

Optional but Highly Recommended Step

Step #6: The Spiritual Step

Incorporating spirituality into your goal-setting process can elevate your journey. Take a moment to connect with your inner self, higher self, or spiritual guides and ask for guidance related to your goal. Trust and listen to your intuition, as it can provide insightful messages to assist you in achieving your objectives. By inviting this spiritual connection, you allow the universe to support your efforts.

Remember to trust in the process and have faith that everything will work out in your favour. With a spiritual connection, you can tap into a higher power to help you create the reality you desire. Embrace this opportunity to connect with your inner wisdom and the divine power within you, and watch the magic unfold as you reach your goal.

Reflection

Take a moment to ponder the importance of acknowledging your accomplishments and integrating spirituality into your goal-setting process. Reflect on how these practices can enhance your personal growth and contribute to the realisation of your dreams.

....

....

....

....

....

....

....

....

....

....

....

....

....

Chapter 6

BUILDING POSITIVE RELATIONSHIPS

As I reminisced about the relationships that have shaped my life, I couldn't help but reflect on their profound influence on my personal growth. A particularly impactful memory was when I was struggling with self-doubt during my career transition. Thankfully, my close friends and mentors encouraged me to believe in my potential, and their unwavering support propelled me to take a leap of faith. This experience taught me the importance of nurturing positive relationships and surrounding ourselves with people who uplift, support, and inspire us.

Building and maintaining positive relationships is a vital component of personal growth and development. These connections come in various forms, each with the power to shape our beliefs, attitudes, and behaviours. By choosing to engage with people who value, encourage, and motivate us, we can cultivate an environment conducive to healthy habits, positive self-esteem, and a sense of purpose.

Positive relationships offer a sense of belonging, enabling us to navigate life's obstacles with resilience and grace. On the flip side, negative relationships can hinder our personal growth, leaving us feeling drained, anxious, and insecure. Recognising and addressing these unhealthy connections is crucial to preserving our well-being and personal growth. By taking steps to repair or end toxic relationships, we empower ourselves to create a support system that nurtures our true potential.

Energy Givers and Energy Drainers: Identifying the People Who Impact Your Life

The people in our lives can significantly influence our well-being and personal growth. Understanding the difference between energy givers and energy drainers is crucial to building positive relationships and gaining success.

Energy Givers: These individuals inspire, support, and uplift us, leaving us feeling refreshed and motivated. They actively listen, empathise, and engage in positive, growth-oriented conversations. For instance, a friend who consistently offers encouragement and thoughtful advice can be considered an energy giver.

Energy Drainers: On the other hand, energy drainers deplete our energy with negative or critical conversations, making us feel bad about situations or ourselves. They may exhibit negative body language, such as avoiding eye contact or closed posture, creating an uncomfortable atmosphere. For example, a colleague who constantly complains about work can be an energy drainer.

Identifying energy givers and energy drainers requires paying attention to their body language, conversation style, and how they make you feel. Energy givers usually display positive body language, engage in open and uplifting conversations, and leave you feeling inspired and rejuvenated. Conversely, interactions with energy drainers often feel draining, accompanied by negative body language and demotivating conversations.

Once identified, setting boundaries with energy drainers and limiting time spent with them is essential. Surrounding yourself with positive, inspiring people will free up energy for more meaningful interactions, improving your emotional state.

As you reflect on your personal relationships, consider prioritising those that elevate your spirit and promote personal growth, leading to a happier and more fulfilling life.

Building Positive Relationships Through Kindness and Empathy

One of the most powerful ways to foster strong, meaningful connections is by practicing kindness and empathy in our interactions with others. By treating people with respect and compassion, we can cultivate trust, boost our mental well-being, and create a sense of belonging that brings profound satisfaction to our lives.

When we demonstrate kindness and empathy, we establish a foundation of trust and safety that encourages others to confide in us and deepen our relationships. This trust fosters intimacy and closeness, enriching our lives with bonds that stand the test of time.

Moreover, research has shown that the practice of kindness and compassion can significantly improve our mental and emotional health. Focusing on the well-being of others instills a sense of warmth and positivity that reduces stress and anxiety while simultaneously lifting our mood.

The connections we forge with others also provide us with a sense of community and purpose that brings meaning to our lives. By nurturing these relationships, we create a network of support that bolsters us during life's challenges and celebrates with us during times of triumph.

To experience the transformative power of kindness and empathy in your own life, start by making a conscious effort to listen attentively, appreciate different perspectives, and understand the feelings of those around you. Celebrate their successes and offer support during their hardships. Remember that even the smallest acts of kindness can create a ripple effect, spreading positivity throughout the world.

By embracing the values of kindness and empathy, we not only strengthen our relationships but also contribute to our personal growth and well-being. As Mark Twain so eloquently stated, "Kindness is the language which the deaf can hear and the blind can see." So, let's be the change we wish to see in the world and watch the magic unfold as our relationships flourish.

EFFECTIVE COMMUNICATION - THE CORNERSTONE OF RELATIONSHIPS

Effective communication is a fundamental tool in creating positive relationships in all areas of your life. From personal to professional relationships, the way you communicate with others can make a significant impact on the outcome of any interaction. It is not only a matter of what you say but how you say it that is essential.

When I was younger, I was known for my sassy attitude, quick wit and sometimes sharp tongue. I wanted to make a point and I wanted to be heard, but I wasn't always paying attention to how my words were coming across. That's when my mother would step in with her wise advice. "It isn't what you say, it is how you say it, I know what you mean because I know you but other people wouldn't" she would say with a smile.

At first, I didn't quite understand what she meant. But over time, I began to realise that effective communication is not just about the words we choose, but also about the tone, body language, and context we use. Building positive relationships requires us to be mindful of how we communicate, so that our intentions are clear and our message is received in a positive way. So, as my mother always said, "You should record yourself to really understand how you come across and work on improving your communication skills". I know my mother just wanted me to have the best chance in life to build positive relationships with others.

When I first started full-time work at a banking call centre, I took my mother's advice to heart. I recognised that fostering positive relationships with colleagues and management was crucial for success in my career, and effective communication was key to achieving this. In order to make a great impression and build strong connections, I focused on the following aspects:

- **Active listening**: I paid close attention to my colleagues' and managers' input, ensuring that I understood their perspectives and concerns.

- **Clear and concise communication**: I expressed my thoughts and ideas in a straightforward manner to avoid misunderstandings and maintain efficiency in the workplace.

- **Positive language**: I made a conscious effort to use positive language and provide constructive feedback, which contributed to a supportive work environment.

- **Seeking feedback**: By actively seeking feedback from my managers and coworkers, I demonstrated my willingness to learn and grow within my role.

- **Professionalism**: Maintaining a professional demeanour in all my interactions showed my commitment to the company's success and helped me establish trust with my colleagues and management.

By following my mother's advice and honing my communication skills, I was able to build positive relationships with my colleagues and management. These connections played a significant role in my career growth and made my work experience more enjoyable.

In the last 10 years after this, my mother's wisdom served as a guiding light and I have evolved in my understanding of effective communication and discovered more about my communication style. As I overcame my nerves around people and became less defensive both personally and professionally, I learned that as I improved my communication style, my relationships improved as well.

Picture yourself walking into a crowded room, surrounded by people you don't know. This used to be a daunting experience for me, but I learned that effective communication is the key to building successful relationships in all areas of life. Suddenly, someone catches my eye - I feel drawn to them, and I want to learn more. But where do I start? It can be as simple as a smile or a friendly nod, followed by a question to get the conversation going but I used to freeze.

Effective Communication: The Art of Building Relationships

Throughout my years of experience, I've come to realise that effective communication is the cornerstone of any successful relationship, especially romantic ones. By expressing your feelings and openly discussing expectations, you can create a deeper connection with your partner. However, it's not just about talking— empathetic listening is equally crucial in fostering trust and respect.

I remember my first date with my partner. We'd met through a mutual friend, and though I was excited to learn more about them, I struggled with effective communication. As I sat there, nervous and unsure of what to say, the silence became unbearable. But I knew that if I wanted this to go any further, I had to try. I took a deep breath and asked a question. To my surprise, they responded with enthusiasm, and the conversation started flowing naturally.

That first date taught me the importance of effective communication in building relationships. It's not just about the words you use, but also about being present and actively listening. This connection we established has continued to grow over time.

I've come to see effective communication as an art that takes practice and patience.

I've also learned that clear communication is crucial in the realm of finances, as clear and accurate communication with investors, customers, and stakeholders is essential for building strong relationships that can impact business growth.

Effective communication has a significant impact on all areas of our lives, from personal to professional. It's about listening, understanding, and building connections. By being mindful of your communication style and adapting to different situations, you can improve relationships and achieve greater success.

Let's consider a scenario: You've been planning a weekend spa getaway with a close friend for months, but as the date nears, your friend becomes distant and unresponsive. You start to worry they've changed their mind or are upset with you.

In this situation, effective communication is vital. Instead of making assumptions, reach out and ask your friend if everything is alright. Be honest about your concerns and give them the chance to share their thoughts and feelings. By actively listening, you might discover they're dealing with personal issues that have been overwhelming. Your empathy can help them feel heard and valued, strengthening your bond.

Open and clear communication helps you find solutions together, building a positive and healthy relationship. By maintaining honest and open dialogue, you can continue to create lasting memories.

In conclusion, effective communication is the foundation of successful relationships, both personal and professional. Developing these skills can be challenging, but the result is a lifetime of positive relationships and personal growth, leading to professional success.

The Power of Encouragement

Building positive relationships relies on key elements like encouragement and setting a positive example. These aspects make all the difference in fostering healthy connections with others.

When we encourage others, we plant seeds of positivity, motivation, and confidence. Encouraging words provide the boost people need to pursue their goals, especially during challenging times. Imagine working on a project without any support—it can feel demotivating and draining. However, when someone expresses genuine belief in you, it inspires you to keep going despite difficulties.

Setting a positive example creates a ripple effect in our lives. By role modelling positive attitudes and behaviours, we inspire others to follow suit. Remember looking up to someone you admired as you were growing up? The same applies at this point in life too. People who witness positive behaviours are more likely to adopt them, enriching their social relationships. Your positive influence extends beyond your life, impacting those around you.

People are drawn to those who make them feel seen, heard, and valued. Practicing encouragement and positive modelling demonstrates your care for others' well-being, leading to reciprocal feelings. Strong, authentic relationships based on mutual concern and respect develop when we connect meaningfully. Spreading positivity, kindness, and empathy in daily interactions helps create these deep connections, enriching our lives.
By focusing on encouragement and being a positive role model, you can build lasting, fulfilling relationships while contributing to the well-being of others. Embrace these

powerful practices, and watch your personal and professional connections flourish.

Nurturing Change: Scenario

Imagine this situation: Your friend confides in you their desire to lead a healthier lifestyle. They admire your discipline and seek advice on starting their fitness journey. This is a perfect opportunity to support them by offering encouragement and setting a positive example.

You begin by attentively listening to their aspirations. You express belief in their capability to achieve their goals and share your personal journey, including challenges and successes. You emphasise that getting into shape is a process achievable through mindset and consistent effort, assuring them of your support throughout their journey.

Next, you become a role model for healthy living. You invite them to join your workouts, demonstrate exercises, and discuss nutrition and hydration. You explain the importance of consistency and small changes leading to lasting improvements.

As your friend stays on their fitness journey, you remain a source of encouragement and positivity. You celebrate their victories, big or small, and help them navigate setbacks. You remind them of their capabilities and your unwavering support.

Through your example, your friend learns that getting into shape is a holistic journey involving physical, mental, and emotional growth. Building a healthier body requires openness to new experiences, consistency, and a positive attitude. By being a positive influence, you inspire meaningful change in your friend and create a strong bond.

In conclusion, encouragement and positive modelling are powerful tools in fostering relationships where individuals feel supported, valued, and cared for. While building strong connections takes time and effort, integrating these practices into your daily life will lead to more fulfilling interactions. By embodying the change, you wish to see in others, you pave the way for thriving relationships.

Now, consider someone in your life who could benefit from your encouragement and example. How can you actively listen to their desires for change and acknowledge their aspirations? What actions can you take to be a positive role model? How will you celebrate their achievements and support them during setbacks? Remember, being a positive influence benefits both the individual you inspire and your own sense of fulfilment. Start making a difference today by being the change you wish to see in others.

Establishing Boundaries

Boundaries play a crucial role in cultivating positive relationships. By setting them, you empower yourself to be authentic and true to your values while protecting yourself from harm. Surprisingly, boundaries help us develop deeper and more satisfying connections with those around us.

Without boundaries, you may feel unsure of what to say or do, leading to anxiety, stress, and resentment. By establishing clear boundaries, you prevent others from making decisions for you and steer clear of unwanted situations.

Setting boundaries is not about being selfish or unapproachable; it's about communicating your needs and desires respectfully. Once boundaries are set, you can foster mutually respectful relationships based on trust, respect, and appreciation.

Learning to say "no" is an essential aspect of boundary-setting. Saying "no" communicates that you value your time and energy, encouraging others not to take you for granted. I learned this the hard way as a former people-pleaser. Saying yes to everything left me feeling depleted, resentful, and like a doormat for others. It took me time to realise that setting boundaries is necessary for building stronger, more positive relationships. Saying "no" respectfully and kindly shows self-respect, preventing feelings of resentment and depletion.

Remember, boundaries protect you while allowing others to respect and appreciate your true self. They enable trust and mutual understanding, forming deep connections based on shared experiences and common goals.

So, start setting boundaries and experience the positive impact they have on your relationships. Embrace the power of saying "no," and watch as your connections become stronger and more fulfilling.

Strengthening Relationships Through Boundaries: Kathryn's Story

Meet Kathryn, a successful and busy woman who loves her mother dearly. However, she often feels overwhelmed by her mother's overbearing nature, constantly rearranging her life to accommodate her mother's demands. Kathryn fears that saying "no" might result in losing touch with her mother, who only seems to reach out when she needs something.

A friend introduces Kathryn to the concept of boundaries and their role in fostering healthy relationships. Boundaries define what you are and aren't willing to tolerate in your relationships. Setting boundaries can lead to better communication and more positive connections in the long run.

Taking this advice to heart, Kathryn sets boundaries with her mother. She explains the importance of having control over her time while assuring her mother that she will still be there for her. Kathryn asks her mother to respect her need for planning and balance in life.

Initially, her mother resists these boundaries, but eventually understands their value. She begins to communicate more respectfully and considerately with Kathryn, acknowledging her daughter's needs.

Their relationship transforms dramatically, thanks to the power of boundaries. Kathryn no longer feels anxious around her mother, and her mother feels more valued and respected. Together, they build a stronger, more positive relationship rooted in mutual understanding and respect.

In summary, boundaries can be a game-changer for developing positive relationships. By clearly defining your needs and aspirations, you can create a more fulfilling dynamic that respects everyone involved. If you're struggling to build a positive relationship with someone you care about, consider establishing healthy boundaries – they just might unlock a brighter, happier future for both of you. Remember, these relationships can nourish your soul and inspire you to become the best version of yourself.

Cultivating Friendships Throughout Life's Changes

If you've ever found yourself struggling to make friends and establish your identity after a big move or career shift, you're not alone. Many people experience feelings of isolation and loneliness during life transitions. The good news is, it's never too late to start forming positive relationships with others.

During our school years, making friends seemed more accessible since we spent our days interacting with peers in classrooms or on the playground. As we age, careers, families, and other commitments demand more of our time, making new connections more challenging. Life changes like moving to a new town or ending a significant relationship can amplify these feelings. However, building friendships is always possible; it just requires effort and stepping out of your comfort zone.

To find new friends, identify your values and interests. What's important to you? What hobbies or activities bring you joy? Knowing who you are and what you like makes it easier to find others who share your passions. Joining groups or clubs that align with your interests is an excellent way to meet like-minded individuals. Openness to new experiences also helps discover more about yourself. Starting conversations with strangers might feel uncomfortable initially, but remember that everyone shares similar challenges in making connections. You never know who you'll meet or the potential connections you could make by being open and friendly.

Being honest and genuine about yourself and your friendship expectations is crucial for attracting friends who value and appreciate you for who you are. Authenticity is appealing and essential in creating positive relationships.

Cultivating trust and empathy with those around you is also important. Deep listening, honest emotional expression, and willingness to compromise or apologise foster fulfilling, supportive, and long-lasting connections with others. Building positive relationships takes time and effort, but the rewards are worth it.

So, remember, no matter your age or location, you can build new friendships by understanding yourself, staying open to new experiences, and prioritising authenticity and empathy. Embrace the journey and enjoy the fulfilling connections that await you.

Paige's Journey: Finding Friendships in a New City

When Paige moved to a new city for work, she felt disconnected and yearned for new friendships. Despite feeling lost initially, she discovered a local book club that piqued her interest. As an avid reader, she decided to attend a meeting.

Feeling shy at first, Paige eventually found comfort in discussing the novel with the group. To her surprise, she easily connected with other members and bonded over their shared love of literature. They exchanged contact information, marking the beginning of new friendships.

Over time, Paige became an active member of the book club, even hosting meetings at her apartment. The group grew closer, forming a tight-knit circle that extended beyond book discussions. Paige felt grateful for the meaningful connections she had built and the sense of belonging she found in her new city.

Forging new friendships and maintaining your identity can be challenging, particularly when transitioning between life stages and leaving familiar environments.

However, with a willingness to open yourself up to new experiences and staying true to your values and interests, it's possible to create lasting, meaningful connections with others. Remember to invest time and effort into developing positive relationships, as they enrich our lives and provide a sense of purpose, as Brené Brown says: "Connection is why we're here. It gives us purpose and meaning to our lives."

Nurturing Our Lifelong Connection with Parents

Our parents are not just our creators; they are our pillars of strength, our first teachers, and our unwavering sources of love. The connection we share with them shapes us into who we are and who we aspire to be. Building and maintaining a positive relationship with our parents is crucial, as it impacts the quality of our relationships in all aspects of life.

As we navigate life's journey, it's important to acknowledge that parenting is no easy feat. Mistakes are made, but it's the willingness to repair, forgive, and learn that transforms these missteps into valuable life lessons. By acknowledging our shared humanity, we create an environment where empathy and growth thrive, helping us break negative cycles and enrich our lives immeasurably.

Distance may separate us, but the power of love knows no bounds. Staying connected through regular communication – be it a phone call, email, or text message – strengthens our bond and reminds us of the comforting presence of home.

For those without parents, the search for love and belonging may take a different path. Nurturing relationships with loved ones – whether grandparents, aunts, uncles, or close family friends – can fill our lives with the same warmth and support that a parent provides. Cherish these relationships and appreciate the profound impact they have on your personal growth.

The beauty of our relationship with our parents lies in its ever-evolving nature. What once was a child-parent dynamic can blossom into a deep friendship as we grow older. My relationship with my mother exemplifies this transformation, as our bond evolved into a friendship built on mutual respect, love, and understanding.

Invest time and energy in fostering a strong and loving bond with your parents, as it equips us with the resilience and emotional intelligence to face life's challenges. Each day offers an opportunity to cultivate this connection, so seize it with open arms and let the love between you flourish. Remember, even if your relationship with your parents faces difficulties, remain hopeful. With love, patience, and dedication, you can build a bridge that connects your hearts for a lifetime and beyond, enriching your personal journey of self-development.

As we conclude this chapter on building positive relationships, remember that fostering genuine connections plays a crucial role in our personal growth and self-development. The people we surround ourselves with can either uplift or hinder our progress, making it essential to create an environment that nurtures healthy relationships. By focusing on effective communication, empathy, and mutual understanding, we can cultivate a support system that empowers us to reach our full potential.

Throughout this chapter, we've explored the importance of diverse connections, such as friendships, family relationships, and professional networks. Each of these connections offers unique opportunities to learn, grow, and enrich our lives. By investing in these relationships and maintaining open communication, we become better equipped to navigate life's challenges and embrace personal growth.

In conclusion, always strive to create positive relationships in every aspect of your life. Seek out connections that uplift and inspire you, and be open to learning from the wisdom of others. Remember, the bonds we form with others are integral to our well-being and success, so nurture them with the love, respect, and understanding they deserve. As you embark on this journey of personal growth and self-development, let the power of positive relationships guide and support you every step of the way.

TASK

_____

Our relationships have the incredible potential to either lift us to new heights or hold us back. This task is designed to help you nurture a positive relationship that not only supports your personal growth but also fosters a deep, meaningful connection with someone who shares your aspirations.

By engaging in this six-step task, you'll learn how to identify the right person to grow with, set mutual growth goals, hold each other accountable, and celebrate your successes together. The power of an empowering relationship lies in its ability to transform your life by providing encouragement, support, and motivation to reach your full potential.

Step #1: Identify a person who shares similar values and goals, as they're more likely to support your growth journey. Share your intentions to build a positive relationship with them.

Step #2: Engage in a growth-focused conversation, discussing your strengths, areas for improvement, and aspirations. Actively listen to each other and provide valuable feedback.

Step #3: Create a mutual growth plan with actionable steps for self-development. Set specific goals, identify potential obstacles, and brainstorm ways to overcome them together.

Step #4: Establish regular check-ins to share progress, discuss challenges, and celebrate achievements. Hold each other accountable and offer genuine encouragement throughout your journey.

Step #5: Participate in shared learning experiences such as attending workshops, reading personal growth books, or enrolling in relevant online courses. Learning together not only strengthens your bond but also inspires growth.

Step #6: Reflect on your progress and discuss how the relationship has contributed to your personal growth. Share your gratitude for each other and discuss ways to continue building a positive relationship that supports reaching your full potential.

Use the space to write down your thoughts and insights from the interaction. Note what you've learned and what you will carry forward in your life.

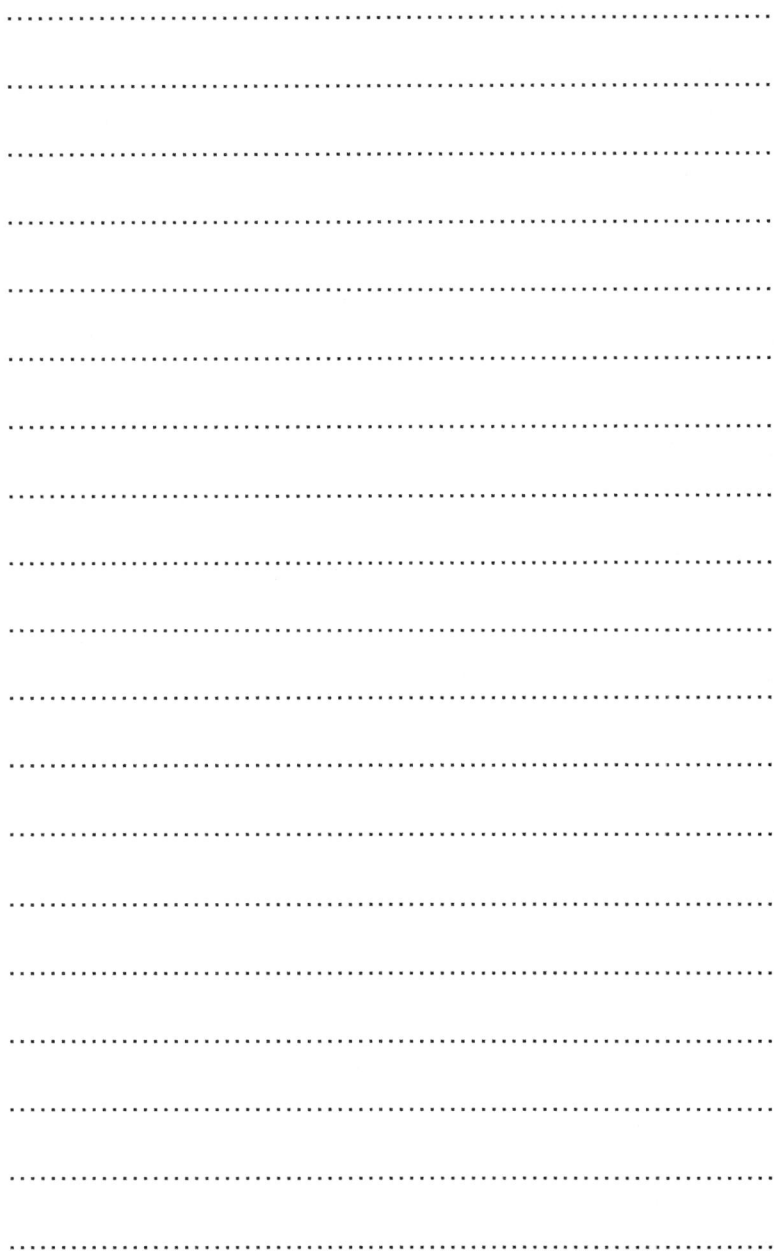

Chapter 7

YOUR RELATIONSHIP WITH MONEY

Money - the very word conjures up many emotions and reactions in each one of us. It can make us feel happy and content, or it can leave us feeling frustrated and anxious. Despite its significant impact on our lives, discussing money remains taboo in many circles. However, it's time to challenge that notion and engage in open, honest conversations about our relationship with money. By confronting this complex topic, we can break free from its hold and take control of our financial futures.

For many, money is a source of stress and worry. The struggle to make ends meet can feel like an endless cycle of debt and despair. Yet, for others, money represents potential and freedom – a means to explore the world, acquire assets, and live life to the fullest. Our relationship with money extends beyond these extremes, revealing our beliefs, values, strengths, weaknesses, ambitions, and fears.

In this chapter, we will delve into the role of money in our lives, exploring its impact on our emotional, physical, and mental well-being. By examining the beliefs and values that shape our financial mindset, we can begin to transform our relationship with money, fostering a healthier and more positive outlook.

As we navigate the fascinating world of money and its role in our lives. By the end of this chapter, you'll have a deeper understanding of your financial beliefs and the power they hold over your life. With practical strategies and tools, you'll learn to take charge of your finances and create the life you've always dreamed of.

SHAPING FINANCIAL BELIEFS

Our attitudes toward money are deeply rooted in our emotional and psychological makeup, influencing our financial situation and overall well-being. To achieve self-growth, we must first understand and improve our relationship with money.

Our upbringing plays a significant role in shaping our financial beliefs. We learn about money management and decision-making from our parents, guardians, and close acquaintances. Their habits and behaviours can positively or negatively impact our understanding of money. Growing up around wealth can lead to a positive outlook on money, while experiencing financial instability may result in fear or anxiety.
Our personal experiences also shape our relationship with money. Losing a job or facing financial hardships can lead to debt dependency, while financial victories can provide a sense of security.

Transforming our relationship with money requires examining our emotional and psychological character, upbringing, and experiences. By confronting our beliefs and aligning them with our goals, we can develop a healthy financial mindset that enables wealth creation, financial security, and personal fulfilment.

Overcoming Financial Hardships

Growing up, I witnessed the remarkable strength of my mother, a single teenage parent who worked tirelessly to provide for us. Despite her efforts, finances were a constant source of stress, and the fear of never having enough money permeated our household. This scarcity mindset ingrained in me a deep-seated fear of money, leading me to believe it was always limited and inadequate. Consequently, I avoided spending, investing, or taking financial risks.

My fear of financial failure held me back and limited my opportunities. However, an epiphany led me to understand that my mother's struggles did not dictate my future, and I needed to overcome my fear. With the support of my partner, I began to unlearn my negative associations with money, gradually gaining the courage to take calculated financial risks. As I educated myself on financial literacy and applied my newfound knowledge, my overall financial well-being improved, and the fear of failure diminished.

If you find yourself in a similar situation, living in constant fear of your finances, know that you're not alone. I've been there, and I understand how overwhelming it can be. However, there's a way out, and it starts with a simple mindset shift: believing that you deserve financial stability and that you have the power to take control of your money.

Next, prioritise financial education. Immerse yourself in books, podcasts, and expert advice on topics such as investing, credit scores, and budgeting. By understanding these concepts, you'll uncover the numerous opportunities available to grow your wealth and take control of your financial situation.

Finally, apply your newfound knowledge in your daily life. Start by creating a budget, exploring various investment avenues, and monitoring your credit score. As you implement these strategies, you'll experience a transformation in your financial well-being, overcoming the fear that once held you back. Remember, you have the power to control your money, not the other way around. Embrace this journey towards financial empowerment and watch as your life transforms for the better.

Cultivating a Positive Relationship with Money

As you dive deeper into your financial journey, you may experience a surprising revelation – money can indeed become your friend. By dedicating time to your financial education and applying what you've learned, you'll create a very healthy environment where your finances can flourish.

I encourage you to follow in my footsteps and make the conscious decision to shift your mindset, learn about financial literacy, and put it into practice. Speaking from personal experience, I've seen the transformative power of viewing money as a friend, and I know you can too. As you progress on this path, happiness, fulfilment, and freedom from financial anxiety will come within reach. Trust me, the rewards of this journey are immeasurable.

If you or someone you know is currently facing financial challenges, remember that everyone's story and journey are unique. But, it is possible to create a better life, where money no longer dictates your emotions or decisions. With determination, the right mindset, and a commitment to continuous learning, you can overcome any obstacle and achieve your financial goals.

Keep in mind that hard work and persistence are the foundation of success. Stay focused on your objectives and never stop pushing yourself to learn and grow. By doing so, you'll not only revolutionise your financial situation but also develop the resilience and confidence to tackle any challenge that comes your way. Open your heart to the idea of a positive relationship with money, and watch as your life takes a turn for the better.

DEVELOPING HEALTHY FINANCIAL HABITS

Our financial well-being depends significantly on the habits we cultivate around money management. Examining our spending, saving, and investing patterns is crucial for understanding our relationship with money and identifying areas for improvement. Our habits stem from various factors such as upbringing and environment, but ultimately, we have the power to shape them to better serve our goals.

One effective approach to consider is the 60/20/10/10 rule. This strategy allocates your income as follows: 60% for living expenses, 20% for savings, 10% for investing, and 10% for leisure activities. Implementing this approach helps you maintain control over your finances, ensuring you live within your means while prioritising essential aspects of financial health, including saving, investing, and enjoying life.

Adopting this rule can be challenging, but taking small, gradual steps can lead to significant progress. Begin by creating a budget and tracking your expenses to identify areas where you can reduce unnecessary spending. Then, allocate a portion of your income towards savings for emergencies and future goals, and invest in wealth-building opportunities that align with your long-term financial objectives.

Remember, your personal definition of financial comfort is unique, and it's essential to establish your vision of an ideal lifestyle. Identify the amount needed to achieve your dreams and believe in your ability to make it a reality. With determination and perseverance, you can develop healthy financial habits that lead to a brighter and more secure future.

Harnessing the Power of "Giving Money A Job"

To maximise your financial potential, why not looking at the practice of allocating purpose to your money. By consciously directing your finances towards specific goals, you enable your money to work for you rather than remaining idle. This proactive approach fosters financial growth and empowers you to take control of your monetary situation.

Here's how you can start:

- **Set Financial Goals:** Define your short-term, mid-term, and long-term financial objectives. Be specific and attach a clear purpose to each goal. This will help you understand your priorities and make better spending decisions.

- **Create a Budget:** Outline your income and expenses to determine how much money you can allocate towards each goal. Regularly reviewing and adjusting your budget keeps you accountable and on track.

- **Allocate Funds:** Assign a portion of your income to each financial goal based on your budget. By giving your money a specific job, you ensure that every dollar you earn actively contributes to your aspirations.

- **Track Your Progress:** Monitor the growth of your savings and investments to evaluate your progress and celebrate your successes. This will not only help you stay motivated but also provide valuable insights for refining your financial strategy
.

As you take on this proactive approach to money management, you'll witness a significant shift in your financial landscape. Your goals will become more achievable, and you'll experience a greater sense of control and confidence in your ability to manage your finances effectively.

Understanding and Overcoming the Scarcity Mindset

Living month to month often leads to a scarcity mindset, a belief that there's never enough money. This mentality can result in various detrimental behaviours, such as:

- **Fear of spending or investing:** You might hesitate to spend or invest the little money you have, fearing it will never come back to you.
- **Resentment towards bills:** Despite the services bills provide, you may feel resentful paying them due to the perceived drain on your limited resources.

- **A belief that money isn't meant for you:** You might struggle with the idea that wealth and financial stability aren't attainable or intended for you.
- **Reluctance to be generous:** A constant survival mindset can hinder your ability to share with others, as you worry about your own financial security.

Recognising these signs of a scarcity mindset is the first step towards change. To reframe your thinking and cultivate an abundance mindset, consider the following strategies:

- **Practice gratitude:** Appreciate the resources you have and the services your money provides.
- **Adopt a long-term perspective:** Understand that investing in your future can yield greater financial stability and growth.
- **Develop a positive money mindset:** Believe that you're capable of achieving financial success and deserve the opportunities that come with it.
- **Embrace generosity:** Cultivate a sense of abundance by sharing with others when possible, without compromising your own financial well-being.

By addressing the root causes of a scarcity mindset and actively working on developing an abundance mentality, you can overcome financial constraints and build a more prosperous future.

Conquering the Scarcity Mindset: James' Journey

James, a kind-hearted and devoted family man, had always placed his loved ones' needs above his own. This selflessness, however noble, had a downside. Despite possessing valuable skills and a strong work ethic, James' lack of self-belief held him captive in a cycle of low-paying jobs. He yearned to provide his family with better experiences yet remained trapped within self-imposed boundaries, convinced he didn't deserve more.

Deep down, James dreamed of achieving financial freedom and creating lasting memories with his family. However, his negative self-perception fuelled a fear of change and the unknown, paralysing him from taking up new opportunities. James found himself stuck in a never-ending loop of working overtime and sacrificing precious moments with his loved ones.

Through self-reflection, James uncovered the root cause of his limitations – a deep-seated belief that he wasn't worthy of a more fulfilling and prosperous life. Recognising this mental hurdle, James knew it was time for a change. He mustered the courage to confront his fears and challenge his self-doubt.

Going forward with an abundance mindset, James actually changed his mindset, leaned into his skills and experience and felt worthy enough to build his own business. The road to success was riddled with obstacles for him, but James' unwavering determination propelled him forward. His business began to thrive, providing not only financial security but also a profound sense of purpose and accomplishment.

As James' self-confidence grew, new opportunities came about for him, leading to further personal and professional growth. With so much pride, he finally achieved his dream of treating his family to a once-in-a-lifetime trip, creating cherished memories that would last forever. Reflecting on his incredible journey, James realised that overcoming his self-imposed limits was the key to unlocking his full potential and living a truly rewarding life. I am really proud of James.

To sum this up, a scarcity mindset and self-imposed limitations are on the top of the list that most hinders personal growth, stifles creativity, and leads to unhealthy financial habits. By adopting a positive mindset, challenging self-doubt, and cultivating healthy financial practices, we can break free from the constraints of our past and give ourselves a real chance of a prosperous future for ourselves and our loved ones.

Always remember that nurturing a loving, confident relationship with money and ourselves is essential to attracting abundance and gaining a healthy, fulfilling life.

"Money is attracted to energy. Where it feels safe and loved, it will flow freely and abundantly. But if there is fear and anxiety around money, it will retreat and be repelled".

Embodying an Abundance Mindset to Attain Spiritual and Financial Well-Being

Transforming your relationship with money starts by adopting an abundance mindset—a perspective focused on limitless possibilities and gratitude for your existing wealth.

Recognise that money is a form of energy and that our thoughts and beliefs have the power to attract wealth and create the life we desire.

To cultivate an abundance mindset, acknowledge your potential to create financial success and concentrate on the wealth you already possess, rather than what you lack. Remember James' story and how shifting his mindset from scarcity to abundance allowed him to welcome new opportunities and create the life he longed for.

Practically applying an abundance mindset includes:

- **Conscious Money Circulation**: Distinguish between needs and wants, ensuring essential expenses are met before indulging in luxuries. Set up a savings or investment plan to grow your wealth over time, understanding that money is meant to flow in and out of your life.

- **Leaning into Calculated Risks**: Understand that financial growth often necessitates stepping outside your comfort zone. Learn from failures and see them as opportunities for personal development, just as James did when he took a leap of faith to pursue his own business.

- **Patience and Perseverance**: Building wealth requires time, effort, and dedication. Celebrate your progress and focus on your journey, rather than comparing yourself to others.

An abundance mindset encourages seeing your financial journey as a marathon, not a sprint. By prioritising spending, saving, and taking calculated risks, you can achieve financial success and abundance beyond your wildest dreams. Embrace this mindset with optimism, perseverance, and a focus on personal growth, trusting in your ability to create the life you desire.

Exercise for Financial Abundance

Developing a positive connection with your finances is an ongoing journey that demands commitment and introspection. To help you implement the concepts from this chapter, let's explore a step-by-step exercise focused on practicing financial gratitude. This exercise will guide you towards a more mindful and confident approach to your finances.

Exercise: Gratitude Journal for Financial Abundance

Step 1: Designate a notebook or journal specifically for your financial gratitude practice.

Step 2: Daily, note down three financial aspects you appreciate. These can be particular events, like getting an unexpected check, or general aspects like having a steady income or a supportive partner who shares financial obligations.

Step 3: Ponder why you're thankful for each item and how it enriches your life.

Step 4: If identifying three things becomes challenging, reflect on past financial obstacles you've overcome, opportunities you've received, or valuable advice you've gotten.

Step 5: As you continue this practice, observe how your mindset shifts and influences your financial decision-making process.

By consistently engaging in this exercise, you will develop a more positive and mindful approach to your finances, ultimately fostering financial well-being and abundance in your life.

Decoding the Psychology of Spending Habits

Our spending patterns offer insights into our subconscious beliefs, emotions, and attitudes towards money. Understanding the psychological factors that influence our financial decisions can empower us to make more informed choices and cultivate healthier relationships with money.

- **Instant Gratification:** Emotional spending often arises from a desire for immediate satisfaction. To combat this, implement the "3-day rule" – wait three days before making non-essential purchases. This pause allows you to assess your emotions, intentions, and priorities, helping you make more rational decisions.

- **Social Pressure:** The notion of "Keeping up with the Joneses" can lead to unnecessary spending on items we don't truly need or value. Driven by a desire to maintain appearances and fit in, we may resort to using high-interest credit cards, ultimately benefiting banks and lenders at the expense of our financial well-being.

- **Fear of Missing Out (FOMO):** FOMO can prompt impulsive spending on experiences or items we don't genuinely need or value. This fear-based mindset can hinder rational decision-making and prioritisation of our financial goals.

To overcome these psychological barriers, practice mindful spending by reflecting on your emotions and intentions before making purchases. Distinguish between needs and wants, develop good spending habits like budgeting, saving, and investing wisely.

Remember that investing, even with a modest income, can yield significant long-term returns and improve your financial well-being. Be patient, conduct thorough research, and consult professionals to make informed investment decisions. Welcome a positive mindset towards your finances and take control of your financial future.

SAVING AND INVESTING WITH AN ABUNDANCE MINDSET

Creating a positive relationship with money can be a challenge, especially when it comes to saving and investing. However, it's important to remember that even small steps can lead to significant progress. By adopting an abundance mindset, you can overcome financial fears and start building a secure future.

Saving money isn't just about being financially prepared – it's about giving yourself peace of mind during tough times. Every little bit counts, so don't be discouraged if you can only save a small amount each month. Even setting aside a few pounds can make a big difference in the long run. Start by creating an emergency fund to ensure financial stability when your income fluctuates.

Contrary to popular belief, investing isn't just for the wealthy. Anyone can start investing with as little as £25 per month. The key is consistency, as regular investments benefit from compound interest, leading to substantial growth over time. Stay optimistic and focus on opportunity while conducting thorough research to make informed decisions aligned with your financial goals and risk tolerance.

To cultivate an abundance mindset, let go of limiting beliefs about money and embrace your capability to achieve financial success. Set goals, take action, and explore various avenues such as stock market investments, side hustles, or increasing your monthly savings. Remember, every step forward, no matter how small, brings you closer to your dreams.

To sum it up, adopting an abundance mindset empowers you to make confident financial decisions and achieve your financial aspirations. By starting small, focusing on opportunity, and believing in yourself, you can build a positive relationship with money and pave the way for a fulfilling and secure future.

Mark Tilbury

When it comes to saving and investing money, there is no shortage of advice out there. However, one voice that stands out for me is that of Mark Tilbury. He is a seasoned investor who has shared his knowledge and experience with thousands of people around the world. Tilbury believes that everyone has the potential to achieve financial freedom, regardless of their current financial situation.

One of Tilbury's key messages I have discovered from his YouTube channel is that investing is more than just a way to make money. It is a mindset. When we approach investing from a place of abundance, we are more likely to make informed and confident decisions that can lead to financial success. This requires us to let go of limiting beliefs about money and embrace the idea that we are capable of creating abundance in our lives.

Another important principle that Tilbury highlights is the power of consistency. By investing small amounts of money on a regular basis, we can take advantage of compound interest and watch our savings grow over time. I have seen first-hand that this can become a powerful motivator and can help us stay committed to our financial goals.

Perhaps most importantly, Tilbury encourages us to view investing as an opportunity rather than a risk. While there is no doubt that investing involves some level of risk, there are also many opportunities to invest in assets that have the potential for significant returns. By doing our vigilant investigations and focusing on the potential opportunities, we can make informed decisions that align with our goals and risk tolerance.

In short, Mark Tilbury's advice on saving and investing is rooted in the belief that anyone can achieve financial freedom with the right mindset and approach. By starting small, focusing on opportunity, and letting go of limiting beliefs about money, we can create a positive and empowering relationship with money that can transform our lives. So, if you have felt held back before from your future investments, realise it could be that you have not focused on the opportunities yet.

Redefining Conversations and Associations Around Money

Are you tired of discussing hypothetical lottery wins with friends and family, feeling as though true financial success is so out of reach? It's time to shift your mindset and start investing in your future, unlocking opportunities beyond luck and chance.

For those from lower-income backgrounds, the lottery symbolises hope and a potential escape from their circumstances. Believing traditional paths to success are unattainable, these conversations provide a sense of control and respite from daily stresses. However, true financial stability and prosperity stem from hard work, determination, and personal growth.

Rather than relying on luck, look for opportunities to invest your money and time into expanding your horizons. Invest in yourself through education, skills training, or entrepreneurship to build wealth and create a brighter future for you and your family.

To transition from desiring quick money to investing in your future, start by educating yourself on the power of investing. Explore the stock market, property, and other avenues to grow your wealth over time. Create a financial plan with realistic goals and consider seeking guidance from a financial advisor or community resources.

Surround yourself with like-minded individuals who share your drive to build wealth and create a better life. Find mentors and accountability partners to keep you motivated and on track. As Steve Harvey said, "Your willingness to look at the people around you and say, 'I need to make some changes to upgrade my circle,' will be the most important decision you make."

Embracing Money as a Tool for Financial Success: Lessons from Mike Tyson's Journey

Money, in its simplest form, is a resource—a tool to help achieve our life goals. As we've discussed, money is accessible to all and can be a powerful force for good in our lives. However, people often view money as a status symbol instead of a tool, leading to poor financial decisions based solely on maintaining appearances. Remember, it's essential to use money wisely and not squander it to impress others.

Many of us turn to money as an escape from problems, but this is a detrimental mistake in our relationship with finances. Escaping through drugs, alcohol, or partying may seem like a quick fix, but it often leads to a downward spiral of financial ruin. These vices not only drain our bank accounts but also negatively impact our health and relationships. Instead, we should use money as a tool to enhance our lives.

Reflect on why you may be using money to cope with stress or challenging situations. Identifying these reasons allows you to find healthier ways to address your problems and make positive changes. Creating a budget, setting financial goals, and investing in your future are essential steps toward building a better relationship with money. Seek support from loved ones or professionals to help tackle challenges head-on.

Mike Tyson's story serves as an inspiring example of why it's crucial to view money as a tool rather than a status symbol. Despite earning millions throughout his career, Tyson's lavish lifestyle and poor financial choices led him to file for bankruptcy. He was infamous for making extravagant purchases during the height of his career, including a fleet of luxury cars, such as Bentleys and Lamborghinis, a $2.2 million gold bathtub, and even spending more than $140,000 a year for maintenance on two white Bengal tigers he kept as pets. These purchases, while flashy and extravagant, ultimately contributed to his financial downfall. As Tyson himself put it:

"I never got a chance to mature into adulthood. I was living this fast lifestyle. Part of maturing is purchasing what you need and not what you want. But I never had that opportunity. I was just buying stuff because I thought that's what successful people do. But I was just immature and foolish." – Mike Tyson

In 2004, Tyson declared bankruptcy, with debts of over $27 million. However, with the help of his advisors and a newfound appreciation of financial responsibility, Tyson began to rebuild his wealth. He started investing in real estate and even launched a successful cannabis business called Tyson Holistic Holdings.

In 2020, Tyson's net worth was estimated online at $3 million, demonstrating that he has made significant progress in recovering from his financial struggles. He has been open about the mistakes he made earlier in his career and regularly speaks about the importance of financial education and proper management of wealth.

The best part about using money as a tool is that the power is in your hands – you have the ability to shape your financial destiny and create the life you want. So, start making wise financial choices and watch as your dreams become a reality.

In conclusion, our relationship with money extends beyond the amount we possess. It encompasses our upbringing, habits, associations, and spending patterns.

Understanding these factors helps us alter our behaviour and cultivate a healthier financial mindset. By embracing money as a tool rather than a status symbol and using it to achieve our life goals, we can reduce stress, create realistic and attainable life goals, and establish lasting positive impacts on our lives. What an incredible life it can be!

TASK

Our relationship with money is fundamental to our lives. It enables us to fulfil our needs, achieve our dreams, and maintain financial stability. However, many people struggle with negative perceptions of money that hinder their financial success. This six-step guide aims to help you cultivate a positive relationship with money and make the most of this powerful tool.

Step #1: Deep Dive into Your Money Story

1.1. Identify key experiences: Reflect on three significant experiences or events from your childhood or early adulthood that shaped your beliefs about money. These could be instances of financial struggle, observing your parents' financial habits, or receiving money-related advice from family or friends.

1.2. Explore emotions: Write down the emotions associated with each event and how they may have influenced your current relationship with money.

1.3. Uncover limiting beliefs: Analyse these experiences and emotions to identify any limiting beliefs or negative patterns that might be holding you back financially. Examples of limiting beliefs could include "I'm not good with money," "I'll never earn enough," or "I don't deserve financial success."

Step #2: Set SMART Financial Goals

2.1. Brainstorm: List five financial goals you'd like to achieve in the short term (within the next year) and long term (beyond one year).

2.2. Refine goals: Ensure each goal is specific, measurable, achievable, relevant, and time-bound (SMART). For instance, instead of saying "I want to save more," a SMART goal would be "I want to save £5,000 for an emergency fund within the next 12 months by setting aside £400 per month."

Step #3: Create a Budget

3.1. Income: Calculate your total monthly income from all sources.

3.2. Expenses: Categorise and list all your monthly expenses (rent/mortgage, bills, groceries, transportation, etc.).

3.3. Budgeting method: Choose a budgeting method that suits your preferences, such as the 60/20/10/10 rule (60% for needs, 10% for wants, 10% for paying down debt, and 20% for saving) or the envelope system (allocating specific amounts for each spending category).

3.4. Review and adjust: Regularly review your budget and make adjustments as needed to ensure you're on track to meet your financial goals.

Step #4: Track Your Spending

4.1. Expense tracking: Select a method for tracking your expenses, such as a spreadsheet, mobile app, or journal.

4.2. Consistency: Develop a routine for recording your expenses daily or weekly to maintain accurate records and monitor progress.

Step #5: Increase Your Income

5.1. Income opportunities: Identify potential sources of additional income, such as negotiating a raise, seeking a higher-paying job, starting a side hustle, or launching a business.

5.2. Action plan: Develop a step-by-step plan to pursue your chosen income-boosting strategy.

Step #6: Improve Financial Literacy

6.1. Research: Find reliable sources of information on personal finance, such as books, articles, podcasts, or courses.

6.2. Continuous learning: Dedicate time each week to learn about various financial topics, including budgeting, investing, debt management, and saving.

Bonus Step #7: Practice Gratitude

7.1. Daily reflection: Take a few moments each day to write down three things you appreciate about your current financial situation.

7.2. Mindful spending: As you make purchases or pay bills, consciously acknowledge the ways in which money serves as a tool to support your well-being and goals.

By following these steps, you can establish a strong foundation for a healthy and prosperous relationship with money, empowering you to achieve financial stability and reach your long-term goals.

....

....

....

....

....

....

....

....

....

....

....

Chapter 8

STRESS MANAGEMENT

Imagine navigating life with a sense of ease, clarity, and a deep understanding of your purpose in every moment. Picture feeling energised, motivated, and confident in any situation. Wouldn't that be incredible? Unfortunately, for many of us, this isn't our reality. Instead, we grapple with stress – an unavoidable force that can negatively impact our mental, emotional, and physical health if left unmanaged.

WHAT IS STRESS?

Stress is our body's natural response to the demands or pressures we face. It signals that we need to adapt or change our behaviour to cope with a given situation. When we experience stress, our bodies release hormones like cortisol and adrenaline, causing our heart rate to increase, our muscles to tense, and our breathing to become shallow. This "fight or flight" response is a survival mechanism that prepares us to either confront a threat or flee from it.

In small doses, stress can be beneficial, driving us to take action and achieve our goals. However, long-term or chronic stress can be detrimental, leading to various health issues such as anxiety, depression, high blood pressure, and even heart disease.

Stress can stem from numerous sources, including work, relationships, finances, and health concerns. Our modern world appears designed to induce stress, with its constant demands, distractions, and pressures. It's no surprise that stress has become a widespread problem affecting countless individuals in our society.

The good news is that there are practical strategies for managing stress effectively. In this chapter, we'll explore a range of techniques and tools for recognising and managing stress, boosting our resilience, and creating a more satisfying and balanced life.

So, go through with me on this journey of stress management, and let's learn how to overcome the stress that has been causing resistance, paving the way to living our best lives yet.

Managing Stress

Stress can be a real nuisance. It's an unwelcome visitor that can show up at any time, uninvited and unwanted. Whether it's acute or chronic, stress affects individuals differently, and many people around the world experience it in their daily lives. If left unmanaged, stress can lead to health problems and diminished quality of life. But fear not, it's possible to manage stress and reclaim your peace of mind!

Certain job roles, such as doctors, nurses, and other public service workers, put individuals at a higher risk of experiencing high levels of stress. However, it's not just those in high-pressure careers who feel the heat. People living in poverty, facing discrimination or oppression, and others in challenging circumstances may also be affected by chronic stress. That's why managing stress is essential for overall well-being and mental health.

Some people are naturally resilient, adaptable, or have a positive outlook on life, making them better equipped to handle stress. The good news is that managing stress is a skill anyone can develop over time. By learning to manage stress, you can minimise its impact on your life and improve your ability to cope with it in the future.

When stressful situations arise, having tools and techniques in your toolbox can help you deal with them effectively. Identifying the sources of stress enables you to take steps to reduce its impact on your life. Remember, there are many ways to manage stress and improve your overall well-being.

Managing stress is crucial because stress-related illnesses can have long-term consequences on our physical and mental health. Moreover, stress can negatively affect our relationships, productivity, and overall satisfaction with life.

Did you know that chronic stress can damage your brain cells and lead to a smaller brain size? Research shows that those who experience high levels of stress have reduced volume in areas of the brain responsible for regulating emotion and decision-making. This means that stress not only impacts your mental health but also your physical brain health. So, the next time you're feeling overwhelmed, remember that stress management isn't a luxury but a necessity for a healthy brain and a fulfilling life.

Go forth and conquer your stress! Discover what works best for you and your lifestyle, and don't hesitate to seek help if needed. By taking control of your stress levels, you can reclaim your peace of mind and live life that is best for you.

Active Coping: A Powerful Tool for Stress Management

Learning effective strategies to manage stress is crucial. One such strategy that I have found particularly beneficial in my life is active coping, a stress-management method that involves taking control of the situation and actively seeking solutions to the problem at hand. In this section, we will delve deeper into this powerful tool and explore how it can help develop a more positive, proactive mindset and build resilience to manage stress effectively.

Active coping is a stress management technique that entails taking charge of a situation by actively seeking solutions. Rather than merely pushing through stressful situations, it focuses on confronting them head-on. By doing so, we feel more in control of our lives, thereby reducing our stress levels significantly.
Stress can undoubtedly be overwhelming, but the active coping approach opens a new path to address it. This technique is highly effective in restoring a sense of normalcy amidst chaos. By seeking solutions, we regain agency over our lives, loosening stress's grip on us.

Active coping involves taking practical steps to tackle the root cause of stress, seeking help, setting goals, and focusing on achieving a sense of resolution and closure. It is about proactively seeking strategies and techniques to alleviate stress.
Aside from reducing immediate stress discomfort, active coping helps individuals develop resilience, confidence, and self-efficacy to better manage future stressors. It fosters a positive, proactive mindset and promotes personal growth.

Stress can compound, becoming a prevailing negative force that eventually wears us down. Active coping can turn this around, providing opportunities for positive growth and development. It enables individuals to become more adept at problem-solving, resulting in a greater sense of accomplishment and satisfaction.

As a writer working on my first book, I have experienced my fair share of stress. During moments when I felt overwhelmed and doubted my abilities, I relied on active coping to manage stress and keep moving forward.

For instance, when I encountered writer's block, I felt frustrated staring at a blank page, unable to express my thoughts. Instead of succumbing to stress, I actively sought solutions, taking a break, going for a walk, and conducting research to gather new ideas. This proactive approach helped me regain control and overcome writer's block.

Using active coping allowed me to develop a positive mindset and build resilience to manage stress effectively. It kept me motivated and focused on my goals, even during challenging times. The skills I gained from this technique will prove beneficial in future projects, providing me with the tools to manage stress successfully.

In essence, active coping is an empowering technique that can help anyone take control of their stress and overcome it. By fostering a problem-solving mindset, this method leads to positive growth and development. So, next time you face a stressful situation, remember to take action and seek practical solutions. You might be surprised by how effective active coping can be – it certainly worked wonders for me.

MANAGING STRESS DAILY: PRACTICAL TECHNIQUES FOR A BALANCED LIFE

While active coping is a powerful strategy for managing stress, having a variety of techniques at your disposal is crucial. Each person is unique, and what works for one may not work for another. In this section, we'll dive into various practical stress management methods that cater to different lifestyles and preferences.

We'll explore techniques addressing both the physical and emotional aspects of stress. Since our bodies respond physiologically to stress, using physical techniques can be effective in managing it. Additionally, addressing emotional stressors can alleviate physical symptoms.

From meditation and deep breathing to exercise and creative expression, we'll discuss various stress management techniques for you to experiment with. Remember, there's no one "right" way to manage stress. Try different methods and find what works best for you.

- Identify the Stress Source
First, understand what's causing your stress. Is it your job, relationships, or finances? Once you identify the source, you can start addressing it effectively.

- Prioritise and Delegate Tasks
Feeling overwhelmed by tasks can contribute to stress. Prioritise tasks by making a list and addressing essential ones first. Delegate tasks to others when possible.

- Practice Relaxation Techniques

Relaxation techniques effectively reduce stress. Incorporate deep breathing exercises, yoga, or meditation into your daily routine. You could also take a warm bath, listen to calming music, or try aromatherapy. Find what works best for you and make it a consistent part of your routine.

- Exercise Regularly

Regular exercise has been proven to reduce stress and improve mood. Engage in at least 30 minutes of physical activity daily, whether running, going to the gym, or taking a walk outside. You'll be doing something good for your physical health while feeling more relaxed and energised.

- Eat a Healthy Diet

A healthy diet is another critical factor in managing stress. Avoid excessive caffeine, alcohol, and sugar, as they can increase anxiety and stress. Focus on consuming fruits, vegetables, and whole grains, rich in nutrients that can improve your mood and reduce stress levels.

- Connect with Others

Social connections are powerful tools in managing stress. Spending time with family and friends can help us feel supported and connected, reducing stress and anxiety. Reach out for help if you feel overwhelmed.

Talking to a trusted friend, family member, or therapist can help you feel more balanced and grounded.

Remember, stress is a normal part of life, but managing it is essential for maintaining good health and wellbeing. By identifying stress sources, prioritising tasks, and practicing self-care and relaxation techniques, you can reduce stress levels and feel more relaxed, energised, and balanced.

PERSONALISED STRESS MANAGEMENT QUIZ

Although I've listed several strategies for overcoming stress, what works for one person may not work for another. This quiz will help you identify the most effective stress management strategies based on your personality traits and preferences. Answer the questions honestly to receive personalised advice on managing stress and finding inner peace. This will assist you in completing the task at the end of this chapter.

- How do you react to stressful situations?
A. I become easily overwhelmed and anxious
B. I try to stay calm and composed
C. I become irritable and short-tempered
D. I withdraw and avoid the situation

- How do you prefer to unwind after a long day?
A. Watching TV or reading a book
B. Engaging in physical activity
C. Spending time with friends or family
D. Being alone and doing something I enjoy

- What do you find most stressful?
A. Deadlines and time pressure
B. Uncertainty and change
C. Interruptions and disruptions to my routine

D. Conflicts with others

- How do you cope with failure or setbacks?
A. I tend to dwell on it and feel defeated
B. I try to learn from it and move on
C. I become defensive and blame others
D. I pretend it didn't happen and move on

- What helps you feel most energised?
A. A good night's sleep
B. Eating healthy and exercising regularly
C. Spending time with loved ones
D. Being productive and accomplishing tasks

Answers:

Mostly As: Mindfulness and relaxation techniques like deep breathing, meditation, or yoga may be your best strategy to manage stress and alleviate anxiety.

Mostly Bs: Physical activity such as exercise or a brisk walk can help you reduce stress and improve your mood. Incorporate movement into your daily routine.

Mostly Cs: Social support plays a big role in managing stress. Reach out to friends or family members when you feel stressed or overwhelmed. Building better relationships may be beneficial for you.

Mostly Ds: Time management, goal setting, and organisation can help you feel more in control and reduce stress. Identify daily and weekly tasks and focus on priorities. Time management strategies may be good for you.

Finding a stress management strategy that works for you and your personality is essential. By understanding your stress responses, preferences, and coping mechanisms, you can choose a plan to reduce stress and improve your overall well-being. Implementing these strategies, such as mindfulness, physical activity, social support, or time management techniques, can help you manage stress and lead a happier, healthier life.

Transform Your Relationship with Stress: A Recommended Read

Have you ever found yourself struggling with stress that takes a toll on your mental and physical health, leaving you feeling overwhelmed and on the verge of burnout? If so, "*Thriving Under Pressure*" by entrepreneur Sarah Morris might be the perfect read for you.

In this inspiring self-help guide, Sarah shares her personal journey of overcoming stress and offers invaluable insights into managing the mounting pressure associated with being an entrepreneur. As the founder and CEO of a successful tech start-up, Sarah experienced her fair share of stress and burnout but managed to transform her life by implementing effective stress management strategies.

One key lesson Sarah learned was the importance of prioritising self-care. She incorporated a routine that included regular exercise, meditation, and hobbies she enjoyed, which helped her gain clearer thinking, increased resilience, and a restored sense of purpose.

However, self-care alone cannot completely alleviate entrepreneurial stress. That's why Sarah emphasises the power of delegation and effective time management in her book. By learning to delegate tasks and trust her team's abilities, she not only reduced her workload but also fostered a more collaborative work environment.

Implementing time management techniques, such as setting priorities, eliminating non-essential tasks, and establishing boundaries, allowed her to streamline her workload, regain control, and relieve pressure.

"*Thriving Under Pressure*" provides a roadmap for entrepreneurs to navigate the overwhelming stress they face daily. With actionable strategies, Sarah empowers her readers to conquer stress and find success in the unpredictable world of entrepreneurship. By sharing her personal experiences, she serves as a valuable resource for anyone seeking to improve their well-being and achieve their professional goals.

Although the book is aimed at entrepreneurs, Sarah's strategies can be applied to anyone dealing with stress in their personal or professional lives. By focusing on self-care, embracing delegation, and implementing effective time management techniques, you too can transform your relationship with stress and thrive under pressure.

I highly recommend "*Thriving Under Pressure*" and hope that if you choose to read it, you'll find the strategies and insights both inspiring and helpful in managing the stress in your life.

NAVIGATING STRESS IN TODAY'S FAST-PACED WORLD

In our modern, fast-paced world, stress has become an all-too-familiar companion for many of us. Technological advances and social media have introduced new challenges that previous generations never had to face. Let's explore how these factors impact our stress levels and discover strategies to overcome them in today's society.

Impact of Technology:

While technology has revolutionised our lives and provided unparalleled convenience, it has also increased stress levels. Here's a closer look at its impact and what you can do to minimise its negative effects:

- **Constant Connectivity:** Technology keeps us connected 24/7, making it difficult to disconnect and relax. This can lead to increased stress levels. To counter this, set intentional boundaries, and prioritise your needs and well-being over digital demands. Disconnect from technology regularly and practice mindfulness to stay calm and clear-headed.

- **Instant Gratification Culture:** The rise of technology has created a culture of *"same day delivery"*, one of urgency and entitlement. To counteract this, be patient and focus on gratitude. Remember that things take time, and cultivate appreciation for what you have.

- **Sleep Disruption:** Blue light from devices can interfere with our sleep patterns, causing fatigue and irritability. Establish a technology-free bedtime routine to promote better sleep and stress management.

By addressing these challenges, we can create a healthier relationship with technology and reduce its stress-inducing effects. Remember, it's okay to unplug and take time for yourself—even if it means telling the world to leave you alone for a little while!

Navigating Stress in the Age of Social Media

In today's interconnected world, social media has become an integral part of our daily lives. While it has brought us closer together, it has also contributed to increased stress levels. Constant notifications, updates, and information can quickly become overwhelming. However, with intentional use and conscious engagement, we can transform social media into a positive and healthy experience.

Imagine this: You're mindlessly scrolling through your social media feeds, losing track of time and neglecting your important tasks. Before you know it, your stress levels start to skyrocket. Yet, you can't help but keep refreshing your feed, hoping for some sort of temporary escape from reality. It's no secret that social media can be addictive. But it's up to us to take control and prevent it from taking over our lives. Let's be intentional with our usage, schedule specific times to check our accounts, and remind ourselves to prioritise the real world over the 'reel world'. After all, being present in the moment is priceless.

Social media often presents unrealistic expectations and distorted representations of people's lives, serving as a major source of stress and anxiety. Comparing our lives to others' highlight reels is both unfair and irrational, as we're often unaware of the behind-the-scenes struggles that others face. The perfectly curated and edited lives we see on social media are often just facades concealing the imperfections and challenges of real life.

The pressure to showcase a flawless version of ourselves on social media can be overwhelming. The fear of missing out, constant comparisons, and the endless barrage of negative news and opinions can significantly increase stress levels. To combat these negative effects, focus on engaging with content that uplifts and resonates with you. Doing so will help to alleviate stress and foster a healthier, more positive online experience.

Furthermore, it is important to recognise that social media can be a breeding ground for negativity and hate, it is continuously being circulated on all platforms and it is enough to dampen anyone's spirits. If you're not careful, it can quickly spiral out of control, leading to a wave of heightened anxiety and stress. However, all is not lost. A simple way to combat this is to make a conscious effort to engage with positive content. It can be as simple as following accounts that uplift your spirits, be it inspirational quotes, cute animal videos, or empowering stories. You'd be surprised at how much positivity there is around if you just know where to look. Additionally, take a moment to assess the kind of content you're consuming. If an individual or account consistently promotes stress-inducing content, it's time to hit the mute or unfollow button. Remember, your mental health is vital, and it's up to you to take the necessary steps to protect it.

By being mindful of our social media habits and taking control of our online experiences, we can reduce stress levels and cultivate a more positive and healthy relationship with technology.

Navigating Social Media's Influence: The Power of Authenticity and Mindful Usage

In today's digital age, social media significantly shapes our thoughts, actions, and emotions. Comparison and the desire to live up to unrealistic standards are often fuelled by marketing strategies that capitalise on our insecurities. As we scroll through our feeds, it's easy to feel inadequate and pressured to imitate the seemingly perfect lives of celebrities and influencers, like the Kardashians. However, striving for authenticity can be our saving grace in this digital landscape.

When we embrace our true selves, quirks, and flaws, we discover a sense of liberation that cannot be replicated. By focusing on our unique qualities and desires, we can find peace and joy in our individuality. Using social media to showcase our authentic selves not only sets us apart from the crowd but also empowers us to tell our own stories.

While celebrities like Kim Kardashian have leveraged social media to build their empires, we too can harness its power in a way that uplifts and empowers us. Instead of chasing unattainable ideals, let's use social media as a tool for self-expression, connection, and inspiration.

To achieve a healthier and more positive social media experience, be mindful of the content you consume, limit your usage, set boundaries, and prioritise your well-being. By taking control of your social media presence and embracing authenticity, you can reduce stress, improve your mental health, and create a platform that reflects your true self. Remember, you have the power to shape your own story – so choose authenticity and make social media work for you.

The Impact of Economic Uncertainty and Job Opportunities

Have you ever found yourself feeling helpless, anxious or uncertain about the future? Do you find yourself constantly worrying about the job market and your employment prospects? If so, you're not on your own. In today's world, economic uncertainty and job opportunities are a major source of stress for many of us.

The reality is that the world we live in today is vastly different from the one our parents and grandparents grew up in. The pace of technological change has accelerated rapidly, and as a result, so have our expectations about what we can achieve and what we want from our careers. However, while technology has brought about numerous advancements and made many things easier, it has also led to significant challenges for the job market, and by extension, for our ability to manage stress.

Understanding the Roots of Economic Uncertainty and the Changing Job Landscape

Over the past few decades, the global economy has undergone a remarkable transformation. One of the most significant shifts has been the transition from an industrial and manufacturing-based economy to a service-oriented one. This shift has resulted in the disappearance or reduced security of traditional job prospects, giving rise to exciting yet challenging opportunities in technology and digital sectors.

Globalisation has also played a crucial role in fostering economic uncertainty. As businesses have become more interconnected on a global scale, industries have grown increasingly competitive, driving the demand for a highly skilled and adaptable workforce. Many individuals find themselves grappling with the rapid pace of change, which can lead to stress and feelings of insecurity and underemployment.

Why Today's Job Market is Different

The advancement of digital technology has significantly altered the employment landscape. The creation of new digital platforms has opened up countless opportunities that did not exist previously. However, it has also caused a decline in traditional job sectors. The surge in sophisticated automation systems has led to the disappearance or sharp reduction of many manual work-based jobs. Consequently, younger generations are increasingly seeking jobs that harness the potential of technology, as opposed to those involving physical labor.

The rise of social media and the growing popularity of 'YouTube stars' and influencers have further revolutionised the traditional job market. This shift reflects a change in societal attitudes, as more people strive for self-expression, creativity, and the seemingly limitless potential that social media offers. As a result, a range of new opportunities has emerged, vastly different from the careers of the past.

Navigating the Future of Work: Adapting to Change and Cultivating Resilience

In today's rapidly evolving world, job opportunities and economic landscapes are shifting dramatically. A report by the World Economic Forum predicts that by 2025, 85 million jobs may be displaced by automation and technology, while 97 million new roles may emerge.

(Source: The Future of Jobs Report 2020, World Economic Forum)

This uncertainty can cause significant stress and anxiety in our daily lives. Increased competition and the transition to a digital economy have left many feeling insecure about their careers and futures. This stress is not just speculation; it can lead to decreased productivity, absenteeism, and poor mental health for individuals and contribute to slower economic growth on a larger scale.

Research published in The Lancet reveals a substantial increase in depression and anxiety during the economically uncertain times brought on by the COVID-19 pandemic. (Source: Prevalence of depressive and anxiety disorders in the global population during the COVID-19 pandemic: a systematic review and meta-analysis, The Lancet)

While we may not be able to change the broader economic environment, we can take steps to better manage stress and build resilience. By focusing on developing our skills, knowledge, and fostering strong relationships, we can navigate these challenges more effectively. Adopting adaptability and a future-oriented mindset will enable us to capitalise on emerging opportunities and create fulfilling lives amidst the changing job landscape.

By staying informed about economic trends and maintaining a flexible approach to career development, we can position ourselves for success and thrive in the ever-evolving world of work. Remember, you have the power to shape your own path – so invest in your personal growth to seize the opportunities that lie ahead and successfully adapt to change.

"Problems can be experienced as ... a chance for renewal rather than stress." - Marilyn Ferguson

STRATEGIES FOR MANAGING STRESS IN TODAY'S WORLD

The expectations we have for ourselves and those around us can have a considerable impact on our mental health and well-being. In this section, we'll discuss strategies to help you overcome stress in the modern world, focusing on the three topics we previously explored.

Strategy 1: Establish Tech Boundaries

As technology is a significant contributor to stress in today's world, setting boundaries with your devices is essential. Limit your time spent on social media, email, and other digital platforms. Consider turning off notifications on your phone for specific periods during the day or for certain apps. This will help create space and limit exposure to nonessential information.

Strategy 2: Engage in Digital Detox

Taking regular breaks from technology can be beneficial for your overall well-being. Incorporate digital detoxes into your routine to disconnect and refocus your attention. Dedicate specific times of day or week to unplug and engage in activities like reading, cooking, or exercising. You can also establish tech-free zones in your home, such as the bedroom or dining table, to promote mindfulness.

Strategy 3: Nurture Genuine Connections

Social media can be a helpful tool to stay connected, but it can also lead to loneliness and isolation. Prioritise quality social connections by creating opportunities for face-to-face interactions whenever possible. Join a group or pursue a shared interest that you feel passionate about, fostering meaningful relationships in the process.

Strategy 4: Develop a Support Network

To handle the stress associated with economic uncertainty and job prospects, build a strong support network. Surround yourself with positive and supportive individuals who believe in your goals. If needed, consider seeking guidance from a professional coach or therapist to develop tailored coping strategies.

Strategy 5: Emphasise Skill Development and Adaptability

In a rapidly evolving job market, developing a diverse skill set can help you stay ahead. Keep up with industry trends and invest in your education and training. Take advantage of networking opportunities and pursue side hustles or freelance work to expand your portfolio.

Strategy 6: Cultivate a Positive Mindset

In challenging times, it's crucial to cultivate a positive mindset. Instead of dwelling on uncontrollable factors, concentrate on what you can influence. Practice gratitude and reframing negative thoughts to maintain an optimistic outlook. Focus on your achievements and abilities, rather than what you lack or can't do.

While today's world presents various challenges, you can overcome these stressors by implementing the right strategies. Remember to set technology boundaries, practice digital detoxes, build a robust support network, and focus on developing positive mindsets and versatile skills. By proactively addressing these stressors, you'll be better equipped to maintain a balanced and fulfilling life.

TASK

Effectively managing stress is crucial for maintaining a healthy and balanced lifestyle. By identifying your stress management style and implementing tailored strategies, you can take control of your well-being. This 5-step task will help you create a personalised stress management plan to enhance your life and promote lasting change.

Step #1: Determine Your Stress Management Style

Review your responses to the quiz questions and note the answer you selected most frequently. This represents your primary stress management style.

Step #2: Choose a Recommended Strategy

Refer to the answer associated with your stress management style and take note of the recommended strategy. This tailored approach will help you address your specific stressors.

Step #3: Implement the Strategy in Your Daily Routine

Integrate the recommended strategy into your daily life, whether it involves regular exercise, mindfulness practices, building better relationships, or time management techniques. Consistency is key, so commit to your chosen strategy and make it a part of your routine.

Step #4: Track Your Progress

Over the next few weeks, monitor the effectiveness of your chosen strategy by observing changes in your physical and mental well-being. Reflect on any improvements and adjust your approach as needed for optimal results.

Step #5: Celebrate Your Successes

Recognise and celebrate your progress, no matter how small it may seem. Remember that managing stress is a journey, and each milestone deserves acknowledgement. Embrace your achievements and use them as motivation to continue on your path to better well-being.

By consistently implementing the recommended strategies, you will experience a positive impact on your stress levels and overall quality of life. Use this task as a roadmap to create a stress management plan that aligns with your lifestyle and needs. With determination, patience, and perseverance, you can master stress management and foster a healthier, happier you.

....

....

....

....

....

....

....

....

....

....

....

....

....

A Case Study in Stress Management

My good friend Mai, a 36-year-old children's social worker, found herself struggling to balance the demands of her job, caring for her two children, and managing her household. The constant juggling act left her feeling overwhelmed and burned out. Mai decided to implement several strategies to improve her well-being.

Step #1: Determine Your Stress Management Style

Mai took the "You are the chosen one" quiz to determine her stress management style and Kate's quiz responses mostly fell under the "C" category, revealing that her main stressors were related to emotional support and irritability. She acknowledged that her stress management style required building better relationships to create a supportive environment.

Step #2: Choosing a Recommended Strategy

Based on her quiz results, Mai decided to implement strategies that would help her build stronger emotional connections with friends, family, and colleagues. She aimed to create an understanding support network that respected her needs and helped her manage irritability.

Step #3: Implement the Strategy in Your Daily Routine

Mai began scheduling regular meet-ups with close friends and family members to adopt deeper connections. She openly discussed her need for emotional support and shared her stress management goals with her network.

Step #4: Tracking Progress

Over the next few weeks, Mai noticed improvements in her stress levels as her emotional support network grew. She continued refining her approach by practicing active listening and empathy, which helped her manage irritability and further strengthened her relationships.

Step #5: Celebrating Successes

Mai celebrated her progress by treating herself to a relaxing spa day with friends. She acknowledged that managing stress is a continuous journey and remained committed to maintaining and refining her relationship-building strategies.

Results:
Mai's dedication to fostering emotional connections at work and in her personal life significantly reduced her stress levels. Her newfound support network provided her with understanding, empathy, and emotional guidance, allowing her to create a more balanced life. Mai's story demonstrates the importance of tailoring stress management strategies to one's unique needs and preferences.

Now it's your turn to take charge of your well-being. Remember to complete the Personalised Stress Management Quiz and identify the strategies best suited for your stress management style. Implement these approaches in your daily routine, monitor your progress, and celebrate your successes along the way.
Remember, managing stress is an ongoing journey, and with determination and the right tools, you can create a more fulfilling and balanced life

Chapter 9

THE POWER OF SELF-CARE AND SELF-COMPASSION

Have you ever found yourself prioritising others' needs over your own, fearing that taking time for yourself might be perceived as selfish? You're not alone. Many of us fall into the trap of believing that self-care is self-indulgent and that we must put others first to be considered "good people." However, the truth is that self-care is anything but selfish; in fact, it lays the foundation for becoming better, more caring individuals.

"It is okay to prioritise yourself. It is okay to honour the season you're in. It is okay to take care of yourself and be self-full. It's not selfish." - Lisa Nichols.

THE IMPORTANCE OF SELF-CARE

Self-care is the art and science of nurturing both our bodies and minds. It encompasses a variety of practices and activities that promote physical, mental, and emotional well-being. Self-care is an essential building block for a successful life, forming the basis for everything we do.

Even highly successful and influential people recognise the importance of self-care. Celebrities like Oprah Winfrey, Dwayne "The Rock" Johnson, and Lady Gaga have publicly discussed their mental health struggles and the crucial role self-care has played in their lives. By prioritising their own well-being, they have been able to excel as partners, parents, and professionals.

Lady Gaga, for instance, is an iconic pop star who has openly shared her mental health journey, emphasising self-care as a cornerstone of wellness. In interviews, she has discussed her experiences with anxiety and depression and explained how focusing on her mental health has allowed her to maintain a healthy work-life balance, contributing to her success. Lady Gaga highlights mindfulness, meditation, and other self-care practices as tools that help her stay grounded and centred. Her candour has inspired countless individuals to value their own mental health and recognise self-care as an essential component of well-being.
Self-care is particularly crucial when it comes to mental health. In today's fast-paced world, we're constantly bombarded with stressors and anxieties. It's easy to feel overwhelmed and lose control, but by making time for

self-care, we can regain our balance and better manage the challenges we encounter.

Contrary to popular belief, self-care isn't selfish. It's a form of self-preservation that enables us to be our best selves for others. By investing in ourselves, we prevent burnout, improve focus, and develop the capacity to support those around us more effectively.

When we're constantly drained, our negative energy can unintentionally affect those around us. By prioritising self-care and not neglecting our own needs, we show up in any situation as our best selves. Our positive and uplifting energy is contagious, enriching our experiences with others and creating a sense of joy for everyone involved.

Welcome self-care and witness the positive effects on both your own life and the lives of those around you. Show up for others after prioritising self-care and feel the difference it makes—not only will you feel better, but those around you will too.

"Self-care is giving the world the best of you, instead of what's left of you." – Katie Reed

For those in caregiving roles, self-care is particularly vital. Whether you're a parent, a healthcare professional, or any service provider, attending to the needs of others can be emotionally and physically taxing. It's easy to fall into the habit of neglecting our own needs when we invest so much of ourselves in caring for others. However, emphasising self-care helps us become more present, compassionate, and effective in our roles.

During my time working in the social care sector, I had the privilege of observing care assistants in settings like residential and nursing homes. These dedicated individuals play an essential role in society, providing invaluable care and support to vulnerable populations, often including those suffering from dementia. To consistently meet the demands of this challenging work, care assistants must engage in self-care practices, ensuring they're in the best position to provide top-quality care to those they serve. Their selflessness deserves respect and admiration.

Self-care is equally crucial for personal and professional success in all areas of life. By focusing on our well-being, we increase our capabilities, improve focus, and open doors to greater achievements in our careers. It's not about being selfish but rather being strategic: investing in self-care empowers us to become better advocates for ourselves and others.

The beauty of self-care lies in its contagious nature. As we place importance on our well-being, we send a powerful message to those around us, emphasising that taking care of oneself is not just acceptable but essential. This creates a ripple effect that extends beyond our immediate circle, inspiring others to embrace self-care in their own lives.

In essence, self-care is about creating a life that's balanced, meaningful, and fulfilling—an essential ingredient for happiness and health. Its benefits extend beyond ourselves, enriching the lives of those around us. By making self-care a fundamental aspect of our lives, we unlock our full potential and live life to the fullest. So why wait? Start valuing self-care today, and experience the profound impact it can have on your life and the lives of those you touch.

EMBRACING SELF-CARE: A PATH TO BETTER SERVE OTHERS

Have you ever felt overwhelmed by life's relentless demands, as if your responsibilities keep piling up, leaving you drained and struggling to stay afloat? You're not alone. In today's fast-paced world, it's easy to neglect our well-being while catering to others' needs. However, what if we told you that prioritising self-care is the ultimate way to serve others better in the long run? This is the transformative concept behind self-care and its benefits for those around us.

One of the key advantages of self-care is improved mental health. By investing time in caring for our mental well-being, we learn to manage stress, anxiety, and depression more effectively. This resilience enables us to be fully present and supportive when our loved ones need us the most.

Self-care also leads to increased energy levels when we take care of our physical bodies by getting adequate sleep, eating a balanced diet, and exercising regularly.

Being physically healthy gives us the vitality to keep up with daily life and lend a helping hand to others without burning out or becoming exhausted.

Moreover, self-care activities boost creativity, which can significantly benefit those around us. By indulging in hobbies or spending time in nature, we nurture our creative side and enhance our problem-solving abilities. This newfound creativity can be channeled into various aspects of life, benefiting not just us but also the people we interact with, whether at work or in our personal lives.

Lastly, self-care fortifies our relationships with others. Whether we engage in these activities solo, with a significant other, friend, or family members, self-care strengthens our bonds and creates cherished memories that enrich our well-being. Focusing on ourselves makes us better listeners, more empathetic, and more present in our relationships, fostering deeper connections with those we care about.

In summary, practicing self-care is far from selfish; instead, it is essential for maintaining balance and happiness in our lives. By nurturing our mental and physical well-being, we become better problem-solvers, listeners, and partners in our relationships. It's time to let go of guilt and embrace self-care as a fundamental aspect of personal and interpersonal health. Remember, prioritising yourself ultimately benefits those around you in the most meaningful ways possible, and most importantly, you genuinely deserve it.

As Oprah Winfrey aptly said, "Self-care is an act of self-love. When we're kind to ourselves, it becomes easier to be kind to others."

NURTURING INDIVIDUALITY AND RELATIONSHIPS THROUGH SELF-CARE

Maintaining a healthy balance between personal time and togetherness can be challenging in a relationship, especially when living with your significant other. It's normal to occasionally desire solitude and personal space. In such situations, self-care can help manage these emotions, contributing to a more fulfilling relationship. Let's explore the importance of self-care and how it can help you create a strong, happy, and successful partnership.

Being in a relationship can be exciting and rewarding, but it's essential to maintain your individuality while growing together. Spending all your time with your partner might make you feel like you've lost touch with yourself. However, taking time for self-care allows you to nurture your identity outside the relationship, ultimately creating stronger bonds as you come together as individuals. Engaging in separate activities and pursuing personal interests can create richer conversations and prevent feeling stuck in routine discussions.

Self-care benefits not only you but also the dynamics of your relationship. Positive energy is crucial for a healthy partnership; hence, taking time to recharge mentally and physically allows you to bring your best self into the relationship. This empowers you to manage challenges and conflicts more calmly and effectively.

Additionally, self-care serves as a reminder that your partner is not the sole source of your happiness, thereby preventing codependency. Focusing on your well-being allows you to understand your strengths, weaknesses, and boundaries, enhancing respect and understanding between partners. Consequently, this self-awareness strengthens your relationship and leads to a more fulfilling connection.

In summary, nurturing a healthy and happy relationship requires acknowledging the importance of personal time and self-care. Remember as discussed before that prioritising yourself is not selfish but rather an investment in your well-being and your relationship's success. By honouring your individuality and practicing self-care, you create a balanced and thriving partnership that benefits both you and your lover.

Lessons from My Personal Journey: Embracing Space in Relationships

As human beings, we're hardwired to crave companionship and meaningful connections with others. We seek out partners to share our lives with, and naturally assume they'll be our constant companions. However, it's essential to remember that a healthy and happy relationship begins with acknowledging our individuality. I learned this lesson the hard way and discovered the profound impact of self-care in building a thriving partnership.

My world felt like it had been turned upside down when my partner expressed their need for space. I initially interpreted this as a sign of discontent or unhappiness in our relationship, taking it personally and refusing to accept the idea. What I failed to understand was that their request had nothing to do with me. Instead, it was a vital step in their journey towards self-care and personal growth.

This realisation served as a wake-up call, prompting me to reflect on my own needs and well-being within our relationship. I recognised that I rarely put myself and my happiness first. Determined to make a change, I began dedicating time each day to reconnect with myself – from early morning routines and exercise to meditation and pursuing my passion for writing.

I also shifted my perspective on my partner's need for space. Rather than feeling threatened, I started encouraging them to explore their interests and cultivate their unique identity. Witnessing their growth and development filled me with joy, as I knew it would only strengthen our bond as a couple.

By actually adopting self-care and supporting my partner's need for space, I evolved as both an individual and a partner. I learned that a healthy relationship isn't defined by spending every moment together but by flourishing together and as individuals. Providing space for personal growth and self-discovery is vital for our well-being, and ultimately enriches our connection with our loved ones.

My experience taught me that nurturing our own happiness, while also supporting our partner's journey, leads to a truly satisfying and fulfilling life. By having self-care in your routine and understanding the importance of space, we can build strong, happy, and successful relationships that enable both partners to thrive.

Embracing Self-Care Habits as a Love Language for Personal Growth

Self-care isn't a one-time solution; it's an ongoing practice that requires consistent effort and dedication. By integrating it into our daily lives, we can profoundly enhance our overall well-being and pave the way for personal growth and happiness. Developing individualised self-care habits is crucial in making each step of our life's journey truly meaningful.

In the grand scheme of self-development, personal self-care habits are paramount because they prevent burnout and overwhelm, empowering us to pursue our dreams and goals with greater vigour. By recognising our unique needs and customising our self-care practices accordingly, we transform them into cherished, fulfilling aspects of our lives instead of just tasks that we need to.

Most importantly, self-care habits are a profound expression of self-love – a love language that nurtures personal growth and happiness. Self-love manifests in various forms, often categorised into five distinct love languages: acts of service, physical touch, receiving gifts, words of affirmation, and quality time.

Acts of service involve engaging in activities that make us feel cherished and nurtured, such as preparing our favourite meals, exercising, or treating ourselves kindly every day. Physical touch focuses on providing our bodies with the attention and care they deserve, encompassing sufficient sleep, good hygiene, and addressing any aches or pains.

Receiving gifts entails treating ourselves to items that enrich our lives, like indulging in a luxurious bath or acquiring clothes that boost our self-confidence and appearance. Words of affirmation emphasise positive self-talk, employing affirmations like "I am worthy of love and care" to invite self-confidence and self-esteem.

Quality time involves engaging in pursuits that fill our hearts with joy and enhance our well-being, like reading, walking, or socialising with friends. By understanding and embracing these self-love languages, we foster a deep sense of self-love and self-esteem, setting a solid foundation for personal growth and happiness.

Remember, there's no universal approach to self-love and self-care. Experiment with various practices and identify those that resonate most profoundly with you. Welcome the journey of discovering your unique self-love language and cultivating personalised self-care habits that nourish your overall well-being, recognising that self-care is not just a practice—it's a love language that fuels personal growth.

Discovering the Transformative Power of Hiking: My Personal Journey

I've come to discover the power of hiking as a vital part of my self-care routine – an unexpected revelation that has enriched my life in countless ways. When my partner first suggested we venture into the great outdoors, I was hesitant, but I decided to give it a try. Little did I know that this seemingly simple activity would become a core aspect of my self-care regimen.

Immersing myself in nature has surprisingly proven to be a source of rejuvenation and renewal. Walking along the trails, compels me to be present and attentive to the beauty that surrounds me, I find pure solace in the vibrant greenery stretched out. The sounds of birds and the rustling leaves have become my favourite soundtrack as I move further into the trail. With each step, I can feel the stress and noise of everyday life melt away, leaving me with a sense of peace and clarity. For me, hiking has become an escape—a therapeutic activity that grounds me and helps me recharge.

The physical benefits of hiking are equally profound. What started as a leisurely stroll quickly evolved into a heart-pumping workout, challenging my muscles and improving my cardiovascular health. I can see tangible progress on my fitness tracker, serving as a testament to my newfound strength and resilience. Even a gentle hike can elevate your heart rate, ensuring that you reap the benefits regardless of your fitness level.

Beyond the obvious advantages, hiking has also introduced me to a wealth of new friends and strengthened my existing relationships. Sharing the experience with others creates a bond that goes beyond the trail, improving my social life and providing a sense of community.

For those seeking an addition to their self-care routine, I wholeheartedly recommend hitting the trails. Regardless of whether you choose a brief local jaunt or an adventurous weekend excursion, hiking can be an immensely rewarding way to nurture your well-being and foster personal growth.

Furthermore, I've learned that self-care activities should be enjoyable in order for them to become sustainable habits. When we find pleasure in taking care of ourselves, it becomes a natural part of our daily lives, something we look forward to with anticipation.

Approach self-care with a mindset of self-love and self-compassion, as it's not about punishing ourselves for past mistakes, but rather about nurturing our personal growth and healing. Embrace the journey of self-discovery and witness the boundless possibilities that unfold when you prioritise self-care and create a foundation for a joyful, successful, and purpose-driven life.

"Taking care of yourself doesn't mean me first, it means me too." – L.R. Knost

SELF-COMPASSION: A TRANSFORMATIVE INGREDIENT FOR PERSONAL GROWTH

Self-improvement is a worthy pursuit and absolutely one of the reasons you picked up this book, but in the mad rush to better ourselves, we often forget a crucial ingredient - self-compassion. We live in a world that rewards self-criticism, self-discipline, and self-sacrifice, and it's a mentality that has seeped into our internal dialogue. We judge ourselves harshly, striving for perfection and automatically seeing mistakes as failures. But what if self-compassion is a key missing piece of the self-development puzzle?

Our culture places great emphasis on productivity and accomplishment, but at what cost to our mental health? Our inner critic can be a relentless and unfair force, continuously drowning out any positive self-talk or self-kindness. But there's hope - self-compassion is a skill that can be improved over time with practice and patience.

Imagine a life where empathy, understanding, and forgiveness are as easily granted to ourselves as they are to others. A life where we celebrate our progress, however small, rather than fixating on our shortcomings. The path to true self-improvement begins with a willingness to embrace our imperfections, to treat ourselves with the same kindness and compassion that we offer to those we love. Believe me, self-compassion is not a sign of weakness but a necessity for growth, and it starts with asking ourselves some questions and learning to overcome.

Are you sometimes your own worst critic? Do you have those incredibly high standards for yourself that you struggle to meet? Do you find that you often put yourself down, compare yourself to others, or focus on your flaws first before finding any of your strengths? I did too, many times.

Many of us struggle with self-compassion because we were never taught how to offer ourselves kindness and understanding. I'm British, and British culture often rewards self-deprecating humour and punishing ourselves for small mistakes, while self-compassion is often seen as a soft or foolish way to be, but what if we were to shift our mindset and embrace self-compassion as a crucial element of emotional well-being?

One day, I went to visit my grandmother, and as I sat across from her, I couldn't help but admire her beauty. She had always been stunning and took great care of her appearance. Even at her age, she looked more fabulous than ever before. But as soon as I complimented her, she began to pull at her face and neck skin, lamenting the wrinkles that had taken hold.

"Don't be looking at wrinkling Nana," she said, her voice tinged with self-deprecation. "Do you know how much it would cost to fix this?"

As I looked at her with love and admiration, I knew it was time to convince her that self-compassion was so much better than constantly tearing herself down. I gently took her hand and reminded her that she was beautiful, both inside and out. I told her that her worth wasn't dependent on her physical appearance and that the lines and wrinkles on her face were a testament to a life well-lived.

After a moment of contemplation, she smiled at me and thanked me for the reminder. From that moment on, I could see a new sense of self-love blossoming within her, and it was a beautiful thing to witness.

When we are self-critical, I truly believe we do ourselves a disservice. We can be our own worst enemy, and often, our own biggest obstacle to get ahead in our chosen path. By beating ourselves up and focusing on our flaws, we create a negative cycle that holds us back from achieving our goals. However, if we can shift our focus from self-criticism to self-compassion, we open ourselves up to a world of possibility. By giving ourselves the same kindness and understanding that we would give to a close friend, we begin to break down the barrier that separates us from success. Self-compassion allows us to learn from our mistakes rather than dwell on them, to see our strengths rather than our weaknesses, and to move forward with confidence and perseverance. The power of self-compassion is not to be underestimated. It can be the difference between giving up on our dreams and achieving them. So, the next time you find yourself in the midst of self-criticism, take a step back, and give yourself the gift of self-compassion. Your future self will thank you for it.

WHY IS SELF-COMPASSION ACTUALLY IMPORTANT FOR SELF-DEVELOPMENT?

Self-compassion is essential for self-development for several reasons. In fact, it's one of the most critical ingredients for achieving personal growth. Here are some key benefits of self-compassion:

- Breaking free from self-doubt and self-criticism
- Transforming negative self-talk into positive self-talk
- Boosting confidence and self-esteem
- Developing resilience to achieve goals

Are you constantly striving for more success, achievements, or possessions? It's a common mindset in our society, but it can leave us feeling overwhelmed, stressed, and exhausted. However, there's a way to achieve your goals while finding inner peace and happiness. The secret lies in self-compassion.

You might wonder, "Doesn't self-compassion mean being soft on myself and not pushing myself to be better?" Absolutely not. Self-compassion can actually help us in our pursuit of growth and success. When we approach our goals with self-compassion, we create a more sustainable and enjoyable process. By slowing down, listening to our bodies, and taking care of ourselves holistically, we can promote greater feelings of well-being and contentment. This can lead to even better outcomes when we reach our goals.

The Importance of Self-Compassion

Self-compassion is a powerful tool for managing difficult emotions and experiences more effectively. When facing challenges, our instinct may be to criticise ourselves for perceived failures. However, this mindset can quickly turn into a brutal cycle of self-sabotage, leaving us feeling stuck and unable to move forward.

Without self-compassion, we struggle to explore and understand negative emotions, becoming trapped in a cycle of self-loathing, anxiety, and depression. By practicing kindness and patience with ourselves, we can break free from these patterns and develop a healthier relationship with our minds and bodies.
Achieving Dreams and Inner Peace
We all want to develop ourselves and achieve our dreams. While it's important to strive for success, we should also prioritise finding inner peace. With self-compassion, we can do both. By cultivating a compassionate mindset, we create a more successful journey as we pursue our goals.

Lessons from My Own Personal Experience

In my own life, self-compassion has played a pivotal role in personal growth. I used to be my harshest critic, constantly finding flaws and doubting myself. Believing this self-criticism would push me to be better, I instead found myself feeling drained and discouraged. It wasn't until a friend reminded me of the importance of self-compassion that things began to change.

As I started treating myself with kindness and forgiveness, acknowledging that mistakes are part of being human, I noticed a shift in my attitude towards myself and life in general. I became more at ease with who I was, flaws and all, no longer needing to constantly prove my worth.

The Benefits of Practicing Self-Compassion

- **Improved emotional well-being:** Practicing self-compassion leads to reduced self-doubt, fear, and anxiety, promoting a more positive outlook on life.
- **Increased resilience:** Being compassionate with ourselves allows us to embrace challenges and learn from our mistakes, fostering personal growth.
- **Stronger connections:** Treating ourselves with compassion enables us to set healthier boundaries and develop more authentic relationships with others.

Welcoming self-compassion brings a sense of happiness and fulfilment that might feel unfamiliar and strange at first. However, by incorporating this practice into our lives, we can let go of self-doubt, work towards a life full of love, joy, and purpose, and ultimately see your true potential unfold.

Recognising When You Are Not in a State of Self-Compassion

As we pursue self-development, it's crucial to identify moments when we're not practicing self-compassion. Although acknowledging this can be challenging, it's necessary to recognise signs of self-neglect and their impact on our mental health. Below are some common indicators that you're not treating yourself with enough kindness and care:

Self-Criticism

A primary sign of lacking self-compassion is engaging in self-criticism. Constantly berating yourself for mistakes or perceived flaws creates a negative self-image and exacerbates feelings of inadequacy. Negative self-talk, such as calling yourself a failure, is a clear indication of self-criticism.

Judging Personal Choices

Another sign is harshly judging yourself for activities that others might perceive as unproductive or a waste of time, like taking breaks or engaging in self-care. It's important to remember that these activities are essential for maintaining well-being and do not make you lazy.

Physical Symptoms

Negative self-talk and self-criticism can manifest as physical symptoms, such as tense muscles, shallow breathing, and increased heart rate. Anxiety symptoms like sweating, shaking, or nausea may also indicate a lack of self-compassion.

Cultivating Self-Compassion

When you realise that you're lacking self-compassion, take proactive steps to cultivate this mindset:

Acknowledge Your Feelings

Instead of suppressing or criticising your thoughts and emotions, acknowledge and accept them. By doing so, you can release tension and negative energy associated with self-criticism.

Practice Mindfulness

Mindfulness involves focusing on the present moment without judgment. This practice helps you become more aware of your thoughts, emotions, and physical sensations, enabling you to detach from them and regain inner peace and self-acceptance.

Embrace Self-Care

Engage in self-care activities that we've discussed earlier that promotes your well-being, such as exercise, relaxation techniques, or hobbies. By prioritising your personal self-care, you can develop a more positive and compassionate mindset towards yourself.

In conclusion, recognising when you're not practicing self-compassion is crucial for personal growth. By acknowledging negative thoughts, practicing mindfulness, and embracing self-care, you can overcome self-criticism and cultivate a more compassionate mindset, ultimately leading to a more fulfilling and joyful life.

"Remember, you have been criticising **yourself** for years and it hasn't worked. Try approving of **yourself** and see what happens" - Louise Hay

Kerrie's Story

Kerrie, a talented entrepreneur with exceptional business skills, possessed the potential to achieve greatness. Despite her knack for generating brilliant business ideas, she faced constant negativity and doubt from those around her, telling her she wasn't smart enough. These voices crept into her thoughts, causing Kerrie to struggle with self-doubt, hindering her pursuit of dreams.

One day, Kerrie decided to take control of her life and discover self-compassion. Recognising the importance of surrounding herself with positive individuals who believed in her capabilities, she distanced herself from negative energy and sought support from like-minded people.

As Kerrie's mindset shifted, she discovered the power of self-belief and self-compassion. Working on her business ventures, she overcame the fear of failure that once held her back. In the face of setbacks or negative thoughts, she reminded herself of her strengths and practiced self-compassion.

Today, Kerrie is a successful entrepreneur who has achieved her dreams of personal and financial freedom. She takes pride in her journey and loves inspiring others to believe in themselves. Kerrie's story proves that shutting out negativity, surrounding oneself with positive energy, and practicing self-compassion can help overcome any obstacle and achieve goals.

Self-compassion is a skill that can be cultivated over time. Here are some tips for fostering greater self-compassion in your daily life:

- **Practice mindfulness**: Mindfulness involves being present and non-judgmental with our thoughts, feelings, and sensations. By practicing mindfulness, we learn to observe our inner experiences with compassion and curiosity, instead of reacting with judgment or criticism.

- **Treat yourself like you would treat a friend**: When facing challenges, imagine what you would say to a friend in the same situation. Offer yourself the same empathy, understanding, and advice.

- **Use positive self-talk**: Reframe your inner dialogue to be more positive and supportive. Instead of focusing on weaknesses or mistakes, use affirmative language. For example, say "I made a mistake, but that doesn't make me a failure" instead of "I'm such an idiot."

- **Prioritise self-care**: Take care of your physical and emotional needs, such as getting enough sleep, eating healthy foods, exercising regularly, and connecting with supportive people.
- **Practice self-compassion meditations**: Explore guided meditations and exercises like loving-kindness meditations, body scans, and compassionate self-talk exercises to nurture self-compassion.

As we conclude this chapter, remember that self-care and self-compassion are not luxuries but essential components of personal growth and well-being. Put these practices into your daily life to create a strong foundation for success and resilience in the face of challenges. Realise that prioritising your well-being is not selfish but necessary, as it allows you to show up as your best self for those around you. Create the time, effort, and love required to nurture yourself, and watch your life unfold in extraordinary ways.

TASK

As you go through your self-development journey, it's easy to become focused solely on goals and ambitions. However, it's essential to practice self-care and self-compassion to maintain well-being and handle challenges. In this task, you'll reflect on your goals, create a self-care plan, practice self-compassion, and review your progress.

Step #1: Reflection

- Consider the role of self-compassion in your personal growth.
- List your goals and dreams, being as specific as possible.

Step #2: Prioritisation

- From the list in Step 1, select the top three most important goals you want to focus on first.

Step #3: Self-Care Plan

- Craft a self-care plan to support your progress, reduce stress, and maintain well-being while working towards your selected goals. List activities that bring you joy and promote physical, mental, and emotional self-care.

- Identify specific times to engage in these activities.

Step #4: Self-Compassion Practice

To practice self-compassion, learn to be kinder and more compassionate towards yourself.

- Identify negative self-talk or self-criticism.
- Replace negative self-talk with positive affirmations.
- Write a letter to yourself, offering kindness and encouragement, as if speaking to your best friend.

Step #5: Reflection and Review

Reflect on the task and answer the following questions:

- How did you feel while completing it?
- What did you learn about yourself? + What changes would you make to your self-care plan?
- Revisit your self-care plan and adjust it as necessary, based on your reflections.

By incorporating self-care and self-compassion into your self-development journey, you'll stay motivated, reduce stress, and enhance your overall well-being. Remember to be kind and compassionate towards yourself, especially during tough times. Use this task as a guide to build positive habits and lead a fulfilling life.

Chapter 10

DISCOVERING AND PURSUING PASSIONS

Do you find yourself caught in the monotony of daily life, questioning your purpose, and longing for fulfilment? It's time to break free from the constraints of a life built on 'real world' practicality and responsibility, and create a life fuelled by passion and purpose. In this chapter, we'll guide you through a journey of self-reflection and transformation, unveiling the power of discovering and pursuing your passions.

Living a life aligned with your passions is the foundation of a fulfilling and meaningful existence. However, identifying our true calling amidst societal pressures can be challenging, leaving us feeling lost and uninspired. Don't let this overshadow your potential. We'll delve into the process of unearthing your passions and equip you with effective strategies to overcome the obstacles that hinder your dreams.

As we face the challenges of balancing daily demands with our desire for a more meaningful life, remember that you deserve to live a life that invigorates and excites you each day. Refuse to settle for mediocrity; follow your passions and set off on a journey of self-discovery and fulfilment. In this chapter, you'll learn how to set achievable goals that resonate with your newfound passions, develop the necessary skills, and seize opportunities to ensure your passions become a reality.

Accept the inevitable challenges that arise along the path to self-discovery, as they serve as stepping stones towards growth and personal development. We'll provide insights on how to navigate through these obstacles, offering support and reassurance to keep you motivated and focused on your goals.

Are you prepared to reach your full potential and revolutionise your life? Let's set sail on this transformative journey together, creating a roadmap that leads you toward a life that excites and fulfils you every day. With determination and the right tools, you'll be well on your way to a life filled with joy, satisfaction, and meaning.

"Passion first. Everything else will fall into place" - Holly Holm

WHAT IS PASSION AND WHY DOES IT MATTER?

─────────────────────────

Passion is a vital element of personal growth and mental well-being, as it speaks to our deepest desires and innermost needs. At its core, passion is about finding what ignites the fire within and guides us towards a life of purpose and true meaning. Without this drive, we risk falling into a life of settling, where we lose sight of what truly matters to us. This passionate energy can push us to achieve great things, but without it, we may find ourselves feeling lost, discouraged, and disconnected from our true selves.

Being able to welcome our passions requires us to break away from limiting beliefs and societal expectations. It's about recognising our unique talents and capabilities, and pursuing a path that aligns with our values. As we tap into our inner enthusiasm, we become more engaged, creative, and resilient in all aspects of our lives. Our lives take on a deeper meaning, and we begin to see the world from a fresh perspective that is uniquely our own.

During my own journey, I've noticed that many people hold a narrow definition of success. They cling to the notion that a stable job with a modest salary is the only practical avenue for genuine fulfilment. While this may be true for some, pursuing one's passions is often met with scepticism and dismissed as mere fanciful thinking. As a result, countless individuals, including myself, have come to believe that abandoning our aspirations in favour of a reliable income is the only way to achieve success.

Yet, there is no one right way to define success. It looks different for everyone. Pursuing the things that bring us happiness or meaning should not be seen as a waste of time. As children, we all dreamt of turning our hobbies into careers, exploring new places, and creating a life filled with adventure. Reconnecting with our passions and rediscovering that childlike enthusiasm is the key to creating a life that is truly fulfilling and meaningful.

Despite my deepest desire to pursue a life filled with passion and purpose, I found myself strapped to a corporate desk—a life that didn't allow me to make the meaningful impact on the world I so desperately craved. I had succumbed to societal expectations, trading my dreams for mediocrity, financial security, and stability.

However, even amidst the monotony of spreadsheets and seemingly endless reports, the fire inside me continued to grow. My desire to help others refused to be extinguished. It relentlessly reminded me that I was meant for something more significant than a run-of-the-mill existence. Deep down, I knew I had to find a way to channel my passion into something extraordinary.

And so, I took a leap of faith and embarked on the journey of writing this book. I wanted to inspire and empower others to pursue their passions, break free from the constraints they've set for themselves, and find the path tailor-made for them. It was a considerable risk, and I often doubted whether it was the right decision or if I had what it took to see it through.

But as I poured my heart and soul onto the pages of my book, I knew it was the right thing to do. With every chapter, my passion for helping others intensified, and I started to see the impact my words could have on people's lives. Even during the most challenging times, I found solace in the knowledge that I was working towards making a difference in the world.

My desire to help others had given me the strength to overcome my circumstances, and I realised I would never be satisfied with a life that didn't allow me to make a positive change in the lives of others. This book is only the beginning, and I am excited to see where my passion takes me next.

In truth, there's nothing wrong with pursuing your passion. In fact, it's something we should all strive for. Pursuing our passions not only leads to unparalleled happiness but also opens doors to unimaginable opportunities and possibilities. It's crucial that we encourage and support those around us to follow their hearts and pursue what truly brings them joy. They will thank you for it later.

So, let me ask you—has your heart ever whispered, urging you to chase a dream? Perhaps it's music that stirs your soul, writing that ignites your imagination, designing a home or a dress? Whatever it may be, don't let anyone convince you that it's not worth pursuing. Allow yourself to dive deep into your passion, let it take root, and bloom into something breathtaking. Imagine waking up every day, knowing you're following your heart's calling—there's no greater feeling than that. So, go ahead, pursue your passions—who knows where they may lead?

It's also essential to lend a supportive ear when someone shares their passions and dreams. All too often, people are discouraged when they express a desire to pursue something unconventional. But what if that passion holds the key to unlocking a world of fulfilment and success? Encouraging someone to follow their dreams can lead to extraordinary things. The next time you hear someone talk about their passion, listen carefully and offer words of encouragement. You never know where it may lead them, and it might just inspire you to chase your own dreams as well.

Remember, pursuing your passion is not just a road to happiness but can also lead to incredible success and personal victory. Always believe in yourself and go after what you truly desire with confidence and determination.

Passion Over Conformity

Unveiling our passions can be an electrifying experience, making us feel truly alive. Yet, the exhilaration may give way to an overwhelming pressure to follow society's well-worn paths. Traditional education systems can unintentionally stifle our passions, as noted by Sir Ken Robinson, a prominent expert on education and creativity. In his 2006 TED talk, Robinson criticised schools for prioritising conformity over critical thinking, shaping students into job-seekers instead of nurturing their unique talents (Source: Robinson, K. (2006). Do schools kill creativity? TED Conferences, LLC.). This can lead us to question: How do we pursue our passions while being urged to fit into a predetermined lifestyle? Let's challenge the status quo and champion our individuality, stepping into the power of following our hearts' desires rather than merely following the crowd.

Discovering our passions requires giving ourselves the freedom and space to explore. By doing so, we may uncover hidden talents and spark a transformative journey towards self-discovery and fulfilment. Our lives become richer and more meaningful as we dive headfirst into our passions.

Allowing our passions to thrive enables us to fully immerse ourselves in life's experiences. We develop resilience, engagement, and satisfaction in all aspects of our lives (Source: Vallerand, R. J. (2012). The role of passion in sustainable psychological well-being. Psychology of Well-Being, 2(1), 1-21.). So, let's be true to our passions and make the most of our **one** extraordinary life.

Pursuing our passions can fill our lives with joy and purpose. Endorphins, the feel-good hormones, are released when we engage in activities we love, leading to reduced stress and enhanced mental well-being. We build stronger relationships, careers, and personal fulfilment by engaging with the world around us.

Failure to explore our passions can result in feelings of emptiness and dissatisfaction. Self-doubt and stagnation may take hold, increasing the risk of depression, anxiety, and a lack of purpose. However, by cultivating self-awareness and a willingness to seek new opportunities, we can tap into our passions and forge a path that resonates with our soul's deepest desires.

Moving ourselves into our passions is crucial, as they give us a reason to live and work towards our goals, help us identify our strengths and weaknesses, and encourage the acquisition of new skills. Finding our passion ultimately leads to the most rich and meaningful life that we choose for ourselves. The journey may not always be easy, but with passion as our guide, we can navigate the complexities and cherish the rewards.

"Passion. It lies in all of us. Sleeping, waiting, and though unwanted, unbidden. It will stir, open its jaws, and howl. It speaks to us, guides us. Passion rules us all. And we obey. What other choice do we have? Passion is the source of our finest moments. The joy of love, the clarity of hatred, and the ecstasy of grief. It hurts sometimes more than we can bear. If we could live without passion, maybe we'd know some kind of peace. But we would be hollow. Empty rooms, shuttered and dank. Without passion, we'd be truly dead." – Angelus

Growing up passionate

Discovering and pursuing your passions can be a challenging journey, more especially if you have come from a background where passions were not encouraged or even acknowledged.

It's a common scenario - as children, we may find ourselves drawn to certain activities and hobbies, like magnets to metal. However, for a multitude of reasons, they may not be seen as valuable or worthwhile pursuits by those around us. Perhaps our parents or teachers were more focused on academic or athletic achievements, or maybe our peers find our interests to be unusual or even weird. As a result, we may grow up feeling like our passions are unimportant or irrelevant, and we suppress them in favour of more socially acceptable hobbies or pursuits.

But remember, just because your passions weren't always encouraged doesn't make them any less significant or valid! Our unique experiences shape our interests, and the beauty of this journey is that it's never too late to reconnect with what brings us joy. Your path towards discovering and embracing your passions may be filled with twists, turns, and maybe even a few loops - but that's what makes it so exhilarating and rewarding!

Discovering and pursuing your passions is like planting a seed in fertile soil. At first, it may seem small and unassuming, but over time, with patience and nurturing, it grows into something beautiful and bountiful. Many people believe that the pursuit of passion is solely motivated by financial gain. However, passion is not all about the "Benjamins", and it is not solely about the destination either. Instead, it is about enjoying the journey, accepting the process, and finding satisfaction in something that is personally meaningful.

Money and success may indeed result from chasing your passions, but the real treasure lies in the contentment and fulfilment gained from doing something that sets your soul ablaze. By focusing on the process rather than the outcome, you'll discover that passion breeds passion, and abundance follows naturally.

In conclusion, the quest for our passions requires diving deep into the ocean of self-discovery and venturing into the unknown. Overcoming cultural conventions and familial expectations is no small feat, but remember that our past doesn't define our future. No matter how long your passions have been dormant, they remain an inherent part of your identity, eagerly awaiting your embrace. So, fearlessly invest in your passions, allowing them to guide you because at the end of the day, our passions offer us far more than just a means of livelihood, but a pathway to fulfilment and ultimate bliss.

DISCOVERING YOUR PASSIONS

Deciding to go on a journey to uncover your passions is similar to setting sail on a grand adventure across the vast ocean of life. As you navigate the waters of self-discovery, you may encounter turbulent storms, uncharted territories, and unexpected challenges. But these experiences also bring invaluable lessons, shaping you into the captain of your destiny. When you finally arrive at your treasure trove of passion, you'll be rewarded with immense satisfaction, realisation, and pure delight.

Many people spend a lifetime searching for their true purpose, uncertain of what truly sets their soul ablaze. But with the right guidance and tools, you can uncover the hidden passions within you and launch into a life filled with meaning and purpose. So, raise the anchor from the sea bed, and get ready to set sail on this thrilling voyage of self-discovery.

It is so easy to stick to the beaten path, but does it lead to any fulfilment in the long run? Dare yourself to veer off the well-worn trail and explore the road less travelled. Discover what sparks the fire in your soul and refuse to settle for mediocrity and constraint. Dig deep and unleash the power within you, unearthing your passions with determination.

Take that courageous leap into the unknown and embrace the exhilaration of discovery. Trust your instincts and whatever Divine Force you believe in to guide you towards the ultimate destination of fulfilment and satisfaction. Your dreams are within reach, waiting for you to transform them into reality. Pursue them with unwavering perseverance and courage, and live a life overflowing with purpose, joy, and abundance.

A great many of us do find it hard to really understand ourselves to know what our passions are but the truth is, everyone does have a passion. Something that they excel at, that brings them enjoyment, and that they could happily spend hours on end doing without feeling like it's a chore. The key is learning how to recognise it within ourselves and then taking steps to pursue it with enthusiasm and drive.

Exploring your interests

Making the decision to venture on a journey of passion is the key to leading a fulfilling life. However, before you can chase your passions, you must first reveal what they are. The secret to uncovering your passions lies in delving into your interests.

Everyone possesses unique interests, be they hobbies, activities, or captivating subjects. These personal fascinations often serve as gateways to our hidden passions. Take a moment to contemplate the pursuits that bring you joy, the topics that make you lose track of time, and the experiences that leave you feeling energised and content.

Once you've pinpointed your interests, it's time to dive deeper. Refine your understanding by enrolling in classes or workshops tailored to your hobbies. If a subject sparks your curiosity, immerse yourself in articles, videos, and lectures. The more knowledge and experiences you acquire, the greater the chances of uncovering your true passions.

Never be afraid to step into new and uncharted spaces. Venture beyond your comfort zone and take in these new experiences that have long intrigued you. You may just unearth new passions in the process.

Through exploration, you'll develop a clearer understanding of what brings you happiness and fulfilment. Once your passions have been brought to the light, pursue them with unwavering determination and purpose. Life is too precious to not invest in the things you love, so go on that adventure of self-discovery and uncover what makes your soul sing.

Here is a step by step guide for exploring your interests and help you to discover your passion

Step #1: Identify your interests

Begin by jotting down the activities, subjects, and experiences that spark joy and contentment within you. If you find yourself struggling, reflect on your childhood - a time when you pursued your interests without inhibition or preconceived notions.

Step #2: Prioritise your interests

Assess your list and rank your interests from most to least important. This will help you focus your efforts on exploring the areas that hold the most significance for you.

Step #3: Start exploring

Dive deeper into your interests by engaging in classes, workshops, and other educational resources such as articles, videos, and lectures. The more knowledge and experience you acquire, the greater the likelihood of uncovering your true passions. Ensure that you approach this process in a structured and organised manner to avoid distractions.

Step #4: Experiment with new things

Sometimes, our passions lie dormant because we simply haven't tried enough things to discover them. Make a conscious effort to step outside of your comfort zone and try new activities, hobbies, and experiences.

Take a class or online course in something that interests you, volunteer for a cause that you're passionate about, or simply set aside time to explore new hobbies and interests. You never know where your passions might lie, and trying new things is a great way to uncover them.

Step #5: Observe your emotions

One of the most effective ways to recognise your passions is by paying close attention to your emotions. Take note of how you feel when you're doing different activities. What excites you? What makes you feel fulfilled? What gives you a sense of purpose? These are all clues to help you identify your passions.

For instance, if you find that you feel happiest when you're writing, you might have a passion for storytelling. If you feel most alive while experimenting with new recipes in the kitchen, your passion might lie in cooking and baking.

Whatever it is, pay attention to how you feel and make a note of it. This will help you identify patterns and give you a starting point for further exploration.

Step #6: Narrow down your interests

Identify the top three or four interests that bring you the most happiness and satisfaction. Consider creating a pros and cons chart to help you weigh the benefits of each interest and guide your decision-making process.

Step #7: Discover your passions

Once you've identified your top interests, reflect on which specific areas spark a passion within you. Through introspection and self-awareness, you'll gain a clearer understanding of what brings you true joy and fulfilment.

Step #8: Pursue your passions

Finally, pursue your passions with unwavering determination and purpose. Embrace the risks and challenges that come with following your heart's desires, and don't be afraid to make difficult decisions in pursuit of what brings you joy and purpose. Remember, life is too short to not spend it doing what you love.

Feeling like life lacks excitement, meaning, or purpose can be a sign that your true passions have yet to be uncovered or embraced. Rest assured, you're not alone in this struggle. By following the steps outlined above, you've explored your interests and discovered what brings you the most joy and fulfilment. You've observed your emotions, narrowed down your interests, and ensured that your pursuits truly resonate with your inner fire.

Remember, discovering your passion is not a one-time event but a continuous process of exploration, introspection, and evolution. Don't be afraid to revisit these steps as your passions change and grow throughout your life. Keeping a journal can be an invaluable tool in this journey. Jot down your thoughts, feelings, and the experiences that brought you joy, as well as things you're grateful for and aspects of your life you'd like to improve.

Pursuing your passions can lead to a life filled with purpose, meaning, and unparalleled satisfaction. Embrace your dreams and boldly face the fears that may hold you back.

Take a leap of faith and pursue your heart's desires with unwavering dedication.
Discovering your passion is a unique and transformative adventure that requires time, patience, and effort. With

this roadmap to guide you, trust your instincts and embrace the exciting journey ahead. Why wait? Begin exploring your interests today and unlock the incredible potential that lies within you. It's time to ignite your passion and live the life you've always dreamed of!

Chloe's Story

Meet Chloe, a distinguished lawyer with an impressive career spanning over two decades. Despite her professional achievements, Chloe felt an emptiness that she couldn't ignore. The passion for law that once fuelled her days had dwindled, leaving her unsatisfied and yearning for change.

Determined to find her true calling, Chloe reflected on her life and identified the interests that brought her joy. She thoughtfully remembered her childhood love for the outdoors and the satisfaction she found in painting landscapes. Although she had always regarded these pursuits as mere hobbies she'd left behind, Chloe began to realise that they could be integral to a more authentic and fulfilling life.

Eager to delve deeper into these passions, Chloe enrolled in painting classes and went on hiking adventures in nature preserves. Placing herself in the beauty of the natural world and expressing her creativity through art brought her a profound sense of peace and purpose that had been absent from her life.

As Chloe's love for nature and art blossomed, she questioned her current career and started ambitiously wondering how to integrate these passions into her professional life. However, she was met with significant challenges in her mind. Leaving behind her prestigious legal career would mean starting anew in an unfamiliar field, and she worried about the financial implications that would ensue.

Despite these obstacles, Chloe's determination to follow her heart remained unwavering. She meticulously crafted a plan, incorporating her passions into her daily routine and gradually building a foundation for her new career. Chloe began painting in her free time and launched an online blog to share her experiences, connecting with like-minded individuals and inspiring others with conversations about her journey.

Her commitment and talent caught the attention of a growing audience, and her social media following grew. Feeling brave by her success, Chloe took a leap of faith and launched a business that combined her love for nature and art. She created custom landscape paintings and led guided hikes, sharing her passion with others and building a fulfilling career in the process.

While the transition wasn't without its difficulties, Chloe persevered through the financial and professional uncertainties by starting small and gradually building her new career. By remaining steadfast in her commitment to her passions and embracing the challenges that arose, Chloe discovered a newfound sense of purpose and fulfilment in her life.

Chloe's story serves as a powerful reminder that it's never too late to rediscover your passions and integrate them into your life. By exploring your interests and taking small but meaningful steps toward your goals, you can overcome obstacles and create a life that aligns with your true self, just as Chloe did.

FAMOUSLY DISCOVERED PASSIONS

Have you ever marvelled at those individuals who seem to effortlessly thrive in their chosen paths? What fuels their unwavering dedication and relentless pursuit of their passions? The answer lies in their unshakable commitment to discovering their life's purpose and wholeheartedly chasing their dreams.

In this section, we'll dive deep into the captivating stories of some of the world's most successful and inspiring figures, such as Sir David Attenborough, the iconic naturalist; Cristiano Ronaldo, the unparalleled football sensation; and Simone Biles, the extraordinary gymnast. These remarkable individuals have uncovered their true callings, followed their hearts, and transformed their aspirations into reality.

Join on a journey of self-discovery and empowerment as we explore the invaluable lessons shared by these role models. Learn how to tap into your inner potential, pursue your deepest desires, and create a life filled with passion and purpose, just as these remarkable people have done. Get ready to unlock the greatness within and transform your dreams into a reality that inspires generations to come.

Sir David Attenborough

Sir David Attenborough, the world-renowned naturalist and broadcaster, is a prime example of what it means to live a life fuelled by passion. From his earliest encounters with the natural world as a young boy, Attenborough discovered a fascination that would shape the course of his life and career.

Despite never considering that his love for nature could become a career, Attenborough continued to explore and learn about the natural world in his spare time. His unwavering passion eventually led him to a job at the BBC, where he combined his love for nature and broadcasting, creating a dream job he never knew was possible.

Attenborough's journey, however, was not without its challenges. Early in his career, he faced doubts from colleagues and producers who questioned the public's interest in wildlife documentaries. Despite these setbacks, Attenborough persevered, pouring his heart and soul into each project and steadily building a reputation as a skilled broadcaster and naturalist. His determination and unwavering commitment to his passion ultimately paid off, as his documentaries gained widespread acclaim and captivated audiences worldwide.

One of Attenborough's most significant achievements is his groundbreaking work on the "Life" series of documentaries, which spanned over three decades and offered an unparalleled look at the diverse ecosystems and wildlife on our planet. Through his work, Attenborough has not only shared the wonders of the natural world with millions but has also raised awareness about the pressing environmental issues that threaten our planet.

Attenborough's story serves as a powerful reminder of the importance of following one's passion and believing in oneself. His journey teaches us that our passions can lead to unexpected paths, but it is through exploring them that we can find true fulfilment and purpose. As Attenborough once said, "Passionate involvement in whatever you do is critical. It doesn't matter whether you are a scientist, a doctor, a lawyer, or an accountant; it's whether you enjoy it, whether you are good at it, and whether it is rewarding to you personally."

In conclusion, Sir David Attenborough's life and career are a testament to the power of passion. His unwavering commitment to his love for nature has not only led to personal fulfilment and professional success but has also inspired countless others to appreciate and protect the natural world. As we reflect on Attenborough's incredible journey, may we all be encouraged to pursue our passions and welcome the opportunities that arise along the way.

Do remember, discovering your passions is a process, so don't be too hard on yourself if it takes some time. Keep an open mind, be kind to yourself, and most importantly, have fun exploring the things that truly bring you joy.

Cristiano Rolando

Cristiano Ronaldo – a name that resonates throughout the football world and beyond. The Portuguese superstar, renowned for his blistering pace, unmatched skill, and phenomenal goal-scoring ability, has achieved tremendous success throughout his illustrious career. But what truly sets him apart is his unwavering passion, focus, and drive.

From an early age, Ronaldo's love for football was undeniable. The son of a father who loved football who was a part-time equipment manager for their local team, he kicked off his own journey at the tender age of three. As a young boy, he would spend countless hours playing with friends, honing his skills and dreaming of a future in the world of professional football. Ronaldo recognised his calling and pursued it with uncompromising determination. In his own words, "I don't like to stay in my comfort zone; I like to push myself to the limit. That's where I feel most alive."

And push himself he did. Today, Ronaldo stands among the most successful football players in history, with an awe-inspiring array of accomplishments: multiple Ballon d'Or awards, numerous league titles, and several Champions League trophies. Despite his remarkable success, Ronaldo remains as humble and dedicated as ever, embodying the same passion he held when he first began playing. As he once said, "Football is my life." But Ronaldo's dedication extends beyond the pitch. His commitment to fitness and health is legendary, maintaining peak physical condition despite being in his late 30s. Countless hours spent in the gym, a disciplined diet, and the utmost care for his well-being – all testament to his unwavering dedication.

In a world where countless dreams go unfulfilled, Ronaldo serves as a shining example of the importance of pursuing one's passion with heart and soul. His determination, focus, and passion have propelled him to the pinnacle of his sport. As he once reflected, "Your love for your passion shouldn't depend on how much money you're making from it, or whether you're getting awards or not. You should do it because you love it, and that's it."

Moreover, Ronaldo has also translated his passion for football into a platform for charitable causes and global ambassadorship. His involvement with organisations such as UNICEF, World Vision, and Save the Children showcases how personal success can be a catalyst for positive change.

One pivotal moment that exemplifies Ronaldo's relentless pursuit of his passion was during the 2016 UEFA European Championship Final. Despite suffering an early injury in the match, Ronaldo refused to let his team down and continued playing, demonstrating immense perseverance and an unwavering dedication to the sport.

Cristiano Ronaldo's journey is a testament to the power of passion and perseverance. He serves as an inspirational figure, embodying the transformative potential of wholeheartedly embracing one's dreams. Let Ronaldo's story inspire you to pursue your own passions with unrelenting determination, and remember that with dedication and hard work, no dream is beyond reach.

Simone Biles

Simone Biles is more than just a world-class gymnast— she's a beacon of inspiration for anyone seeking to discover and pursue their passions with unbridled determination. At the tender age of six, Biles turned to gymnastics as an escape from her turbulent past. Taken in by her grandparents in Texas, Biles was quickly spotted by a gymnastics coach who recognised her extraordinary talent.

Under the guidance of coach Aimee Boorman, Biles honed her skills and flourished, capturing the world's attention with her breathtaking performances and magnetic energy. Through unwavering dedication and hard work, she has shattered records and claimed countless Olympic medals, all while inspiring countless others with her resilience and unrelenting pursuit of greatness.

For Biles, gymnastics has been a lifeline, granting her an identity beyond her troubled upbringing. The sport has instilled in her a sense of devotion, direction, and self-confidence. In an interview with CNN, she shared how gymnastics has provided her with structure, discipline, and even therapy, allowing her to overcome past struggles and build a successful future.

What truly distinguishes Biles is her ability to leverage her platform to speak out on crucial issues, from mental health to sexual abuse. In 2018, she bravely revealed her experience as a victim of sexual abuse by former USA Gymnastics team doctor Larry Nassar. Since then, she has been a tireless advocate for survivors, demanding accountability and change within the gymnastics community.

Biles' story offers invaluable lessons for anyone striving to discover and embrace their passions. Her journey demonstrates the transformative power of perseverance and self-belief in overcoming obstacles, and how nurturing one's talents can lead to personal growth and success. As Biles once shared on Instagram, "The strongest people aren't always physical. Sometimes, the strongest people are the ones who have the courage to stand up."

Today, Simone Biles stands as a role model to young girls worldwide, embodying the boundless possibilities that arise when passion meets dedication. Through her grit, resilience, and character, she continues to inspire others to surmount their challenges and follow their dreams. Biles' story serves as a powerful reminder that, with unwavering passion and determination, anything is possible.

Discovering and pursuing your passion can unlock boundless possibilities and lead to extraordinary achievements. The inspiring stories of Sir David Attenborough, Cristiano Ronaldo, and Simone Biles serve as shining examples of the power of following one's passion with unwavering dedication.

Attenborough's fascination with nature began in his own backyard, where he spent countless hours exploring and studying wildlife. This passion eventually led him to become a world-renowned naturalist and broadcaster. Cristiano Ronaldo's love for football was ignited by playful games with a tin can on the streets, and Simone Biles discovered her exceptional talent by trying out various sports as a child.

These remarkable individuals remind us that playful experimentation can be the key to uncovering hidden passions. By allowing ourselves to explore different interests, even if they seem unrelated to our ultimate goals, we open doors to new opportunities and self-discovery.

Moreover, their journeys demonstrate the importance of resilience in overcoming challenges. Attenborough, Ronaldo, and Biles all faced obstacles on their paths to success, but their relentless pursuit of their passions propelled them forward. As Ronaldo once said, "I don't like to stay in my comfort zone; I like to push myself to the limit."

To discover your own passions, take inspiration from these extraordinary lives and don't hold back. Ignite the fire within and chase your dreams with all your might. Using the tools in this chapter know that your passion is waiting to be discovered, and the possibilities are endless.

A *burning passion* coupled with absolute detachment is the key to all success - Gandhi

Passions that challenge gender stereotypes

Gender stereotypes have long dictated the roles and pursuits society deems "appropriate" for men and women. Despite progress towards challenging these traditional norms, we still have a long way to go. Pressures to conform to societal expectations often hinder individuals from pursuing their true passions and interests.

If you're someone who wants to pursue a passion that is not necessarily associated with your gender, know that you're not alone. It can be challenging to break free from societal expectations and face the potential criticism that comes with it. However, it's crucial to remember that your happiness and personal fulfilment are worth it.

This issue is particularly prominent in the world of sports. Historically, women athletes faced ridicule and dismissal, while boys who showed interest in activities like dance or ballet were frequently mocked or bullied. Thankfully, times are changing, and we see more people breaking free from these gender stereotypes. Female professional footballers, world-renowned male ballet dancers, and non-binary scientists serve as inspiring examples of individuals challenging societal expectations and redefining what it means to follow one's passion.

However, challenging gender stereotypes isn't always easy. Society can be harsh and unforgiving, often leading to criticism and ostracism for those who dare to be different. This struggle is amplified for members of the transgender community, who frequently face discrimination for expressing their authentic selves.

Take, for example, the experiences of transgender athletes like Schuyler Bailar. Bailar was a standout swimmer in high school, but he faced numerous obstacles when he came out as transgender. Despite these challenges, Bailar persisted, becoming the first openly transgender athlete to compete in any sport on an NCAA Division I men's team. Stories like Bailar's showcase the resilience and determination needed to overcome the barriers faced by those who break free from traditional gender roles.

Supporting those who pursue their passions, regardless of whether we fully understand them, is crucial to creating a more inclusive and accepting society. Encouraging others in their endeavours fosters an environment that values diversity and individuality. As we continue to challenge gender stereotypes, it's important to remember that empathy, kindness, and support go a long way in shaping a more positive world.

By celebrating the accomplishments of those who defy gender norms and sharing their stories, we can inspire future generations to follow their passions without fear of judgment or ridicule. Together, we can create a world that values and uplifts every individual's unique interests and aspirations, moving ever closer to a more inclusive and equitable society.

Winning strategies for pursing your passions

Heading towards self-discovery and pursuing your passions are essential steps to be living a meaningful and satisfying life. However, it can be challenging to know where to start or how to stay on track. The following strategies will guide you on your path to discovering and pursuing your passions with purpose and intention.

- **Start with Self-Awareness**: Self-awareness is the foundation of discovering your passions. Take a step back from your daily routine and reflect on your life. Ask yourself: What do you love to do? What are you good at? What are your values and beliefs? What motivates and inspires you? By understanding your strengths, values, and passions, you can identify activities and goals that align with your authentic self.

- **Explore New Things**: Once you have a better understanding of your interests and values, it's time to explore new things. Try new activities, hobbies, or experiences that challenge you. Attend events, join clubs, or take courses in matters that interest you. By exploring new things, you may discover hidden passions that you never knew existed.

- **Build Resilience and Persist Through Challenges**: As you pursue your passions, you will encounter obstacles and setbacks. While it's important to push through the pain, remember to balance persistence with self-care. Embrace challenges as opportunities to grow, but also prioritise rest, recovery, and self-compassion to maintain your well-being and long-term success.

- **Set SMART Goals**: Once you have identified your passions, set goals that align with them. Create goals that are specific, measurable, achievable, relevant, and time-bound. Break them down into smaller steps and track your progress along the way. SMART goals will help you focus your energy and efforts and make tangible progress towards your passions.

- **Keep Yourself around Supportive People**: Pursuing your passions can be challenging, especially if you face resistance or criticism from others. Build a network of friends, family, mentors, and coaches who believe in you and support your goals. Their advice, encouragement, and accountability will help you overcome obstacles and stay motivated.

- **Look at Failure as a Learning Opportunity**: As you pursue your passions, you may face failures, setbacks, and disappointments. Instead of letting these experiences discourage you, use them as opportunities to learn, grow, and improve. Reflect on what went wrong and how you can do better next time. By embracing failure as a learning opportunity, you'll develop resilience, adaptability, and self-mastery, ultimately leading to success in your pursuit of passions.

As you navigate the path of pursuing your passions, remember that this journey is an ongoing process filled with growth, learning, and self-discovery. The strategies outlined in this chapter are meant to serve as a guiding light, providing direction and reassurance along the way.

In moments of doubt or uncertainty, refer back to these strategies for inspiration and encouragement. Remember, the pursuit of your passions is a lifelong endeavour, and it's natural to face challenges and setbacks. Use this book as a resource to help you stay focused, motivated, and committed to your goals.

Our hope is that the lessons shared here will have an everlasting impact on your journey, empowering you to overcome obstacles, embrace your authentic self, and create a life filled with purpose and passion. Keep this chapter close at hand, and let it serve as a source of strength, inspiration, and guidance as you continue on your path to personal accomplishment and success.

TASK

Passion Mapping: Unlock Your True Potential

Get ready for the "Passion Mapping" exercise! This powerful activity will help you identify your interests, align them with your core values, and ultimately lead you to your most fulfilling life.

Step #1: Begin with Self-Reflection: Set aside some quiet time for yourself to reflect on your life. Ask yourself a series of thought-provoking questions like,

"What activities do I genuinely enjoy?",
"What are my core values?",
"What makes me feel fulfilled?"

Take note of your answers and let your inner voice guide you.

Step #2: Create Your Passion Map: Grab a sheet of paper and a pen, and let your creativity flow! Start by drawing a central circle labeled "My Passion." Next, branch out by drawing lines from the central circle, with each line representing a different area of your life, such as work, hobbies, relationships, spirituality, or personal growth.

Step #3: Explore and Expand: It's time to dive deep into each area of your life. Ask yourself what you enjoy and value in each category, and write down your thoughts along the corresponding branches. Remember to be honest and open-minded as you explore new avenues and possibilities.

Step #4: Assess Your Passions: With your passions taking shape, it's time to evaluate which ones hold the most significance in your life. Assign a score from 1 to 10 to each passion based on how much it resonates with you. You'll begin to see a pattern of which passions stand out above the rest.

Step #5: Connect the Dots: Now, let's bring your passions to life! Draw connections between the passions that scored the highest and the branches they stem from. This visual representation will help you see how your passions align with various areas of your life.

Step #6: Define Your Purpose: As you study your passion map, you'll notice recurring themes and patterns. Use these insights to craft a personal mission statement that reflects your passions and values. This statement will serve as a guiding light, encouraging you to take action and make meaningful changes in your life.

The "Passion Mapping" exercise is a powerful tool to help you uncover your passions and align your life with your true calling. By committing to this activity and staying open to new discoveries, you'll pave the way for a more fulfilling and purpose-driven life. So, grab your pen and paper, and let your passions unfold!

....

....

....

....

....

....

....

....

....

....

....

....

....

....

....

....

....

....

....

....

....

....

....

....

By identifying your passions, you have taken a big step towards living an enjoyable and purposeful life. Remember that pursuing your passions may not always be easy, but it is worth it. Keep referring back to your mission statement and take intentional steps towards your goals.

If you ever get stuck on your mission, refer back to the winning strategies to keep you on your path. It's important to fill your life with activities that bring you joy and accomplishment. When you pursue your passions with intention and determination, you will find that anything is possible.

Chapter 11

CULTIVATING A GROWTH MINDSET

Ever felt like you're spinning your wheels, struggling to make progress despite your best efforts? Maybe you've hit a wall or stumbled upon a setback, and you're finding it difficult to bounce back. If this sounds familiar, you might need to adopt a powerful tool called the growth mindset.

At the heart of personal development lies your mindset – the lens through which you view yourself, your experiences, and the world around you. Your mindset can either empower you to tackle challenges head-on and flourish, or it can keep you trapped in a cycle of self-doubt and stagnation. Cultivating a growth mindset is the key to transforming your approach to life's obstacles and setbacks. By embracing this mindset, you'll unlock a world of possibilities and uncover your true potential.

So, what exactly is a growth mindset? In essence, it's a belief system that emphasises the power of continuous learning and self-improvement. It's about seeing obstacles as opportunities and recognising that effort and perseverance are the cornerstones of success. On the flip side, a scarcity mindset – which we've touched upon in our discussion on money – is a limiting belief system that views the world as a zero-sum game, where resources are scarce, and success is reserved for the fortunate few. But what about other aspects of our lives?

In this chapter, we'll explore how to cultivate a growth mindset and witness its transformative impact on various facets of your life. We'll examine the harmful effects of a scarcity mindset and how it can hinder you from reaching your full potential. By shifting your perspective and embracing a growth mindset, you'll unleash your creativity, bolster your resilience, develop new skills, and ultimately achieve your goals.

To truly understand the power of a growth mindset, it's crucial to grasp the concept of fixed vs. growth mindset. A fixed mindset assumes that intelligence, abilities, and talents are innate – you either have them or you don't. This mindset can lead to a fear of failure, a constant need for validation, and a tendency to give up when faced with challenges. In contrast, a growth mindset embraces the idea that intelligence, abilities, and talents can be developed through hard work and dedication. This mindset fosters resilience, a passion for learning, and the determination to overcome obstacles.

The primary difference between these two mindsets lies in how we face challenges. With a fixed mindset, we shy away from challenges, fearing they might expose our flaws and weaknesses. We feel the need to prove ourselves repeatedly, and failure can be a severe blow to our self-esteem. In contrast, a growth mindset sees challenges as stepping stones to growth and improvement. Failure is merely a temporary setback and a chance to learn and adapt. This mindset shift can significantly impact your personal and professional development, enabling you to achieve more than you ever thought possible.

As we embark on this journey together, remember: *"You'll never know how high you can soar until you spread your wings and embrace the limitless possibilities of a growth mindset."* So, let's dive in and unlock the power within you!

WHY A GROWTH MINDSET MATTERS AND HOW IT CAN TRANSFORM YOUR LIFE

Have you ever wondered why some people seem to effortlessly bounce back from setbacks and continuously grow, while others struggle to move past their mistakes? The secret lies in the power of a growth mindset.
A growth mindset is the belief that our intelligence, abilities, and talents can be developed through dedication, hard work, and perseverance. It acknowledges the incredible capacity of our brains to grow and form new connections throughout our lives, allowing us to learn and improve continuously.

Understanding a growth mindset becomes clearer when we compare it with its counterpart – the fixed mindset. People with a fixed mindset believe that their abilities and intelligence are innate and unchangeable, causing them to view challenges as threats and failures as permanent roadblocks. On the other hand, those with a growth mindset perceive challenges as opportunities to learn and grow, seeing failure as a natural part of the learning process and using setbacks as stepping stones to success.

Developing a growth mindset can significantly impact our lives, enabling us to continuously learn, grow, and thrive. We become more open to new opportunities and experiences, enhancing our resilience in the face of any real challenges in our path. Our curiosity and determination are unleashed, and we confidently tackle life with an unwavering belief in our potential for growth.

I remember being trapped in a fixed mindset during my twenties, believing my abilities and talents were fixed. Growing up, I often heard that our intelligence was predetermined, and if I couldn't do something, it meant I wasn't good enough. This limiting belief made me think I could never be more than what I already was and if I stayed where I was, I'd be safe.

Most people fail in life not because they aim too high and miss, but because they aim too low and hit."
— Les Brown

My perspective shifted when I discovered the concept of a growth mindset through Eric Thomas, a phenomenal motivational speaker who emphasised the importance of effort and hard work over natural talent. He shared a powerful quote, "Hard work beats talent when talent doesn't work hard," which resonated deeply with me. I realised that my success depended on my willingness to put in the effort and persevere, even when faced with self-doubt or adversity. This meant making sacrifices and prioritising my goals, as growth often demands a certain level of commitment and dedication.

No longer did I believe that my abilities were limited or that my circumstances would hold me back. Instead, I took more calculated risks, I became resourceful and found ways to overcome obstacles, just as countless others have done before me. Eric Thomas's wisdom not only transformed my mindset but also serves as a guiding principle for anyone seeking personal growth and success.

As you reflect on your journey, consider welcoming the power of a growth mindset and the sacrifices it may entail. Understand that being resourceful and dedicated to your goals can help you navigate the path to success. By focusing on effort, perseverance, and learning from setbacks, you too can unlock your true potential and overcome challenges that may seem insurmountable.

Understanding the Research and Views on Growth Mindset

Carol Dweck, a prominent psychologist, is a leading expert on growth mindset. Her book, Mindset: The New Psychology of Success, has become essential reading for anyone interested in harnessing the power of this concept. Dweck's research highlights that individuals who believe in their ability to develop and improve are more likely to embrace challenges, learn from mistakes, and persevere through obstacles.

Throughout her years of research, Carol Dweck discovered that a growth mindset is a crucial factor in achieving personal success and accomplishment. As discussed, the core principle of a growth mindset is the belief that our abilities and talents can be developed over time through hard work, determination, and dedication. In contrast, a 'fixed mindset' assumes that our skills and talents are predetermined and cannot be changed or enhanced.

When we embody a growth mindset, we open ourselves up to a world of possibilities and opportunities. Research has shown that we become less likely to give up when facing challenges and setbacks, viewing them as opportunities for growth and learning. We are more willing to take risks and try new things, understanding that failure is not a reflection of our abilities but a natural part of the learning process.

However, when we are limited by a fixed mindset, we stifle our potential. We tend to shy away from challenges and opt for the safe and easy path in life. This mindset can lead to avoiding certain activities or pursuits altogether, fearing that we might not possess the necessary skills to succeed and could face embarrassment or judgment as a result.

Essentially, a growth mindset acknowledges that our current reality or circumstances don't define our future. Instead, it focuses on the endless possibilities that lie ahead when we invest effort and dedication. Understanding that if you feel like you don't have the ability, it's time to like we've discussed before to "put a cap on it" – meaning, shift your focus to your capability rather than your limitations. Remember, you are more capable than you've ever thought before, and with a growth mindset, you can transform your potential into reality.

"The passion for stretching yourself and sticking to it, even (or especially) when it's not going well, is the hallmark of the growth mindset. This is the mindset that allows people to thrive during some of the most challenging times in their lives." – Carol Dweck

Throughout history, philosophers have acknowledged the remarkable power of a growth mindset. They understood that by viewing our abilities and intelligence as flexible, rather than fixed, we unlock an extraordinary potential for personal growth and development. Perhaps one of the most well-known philosophers in this regard is Aristotle, who believed that through hard work and self-reflection, we can continually improve ourselves. He argued that the key to cultivating a growth mindset is to focus on our virtues and character, rather than simply our talents or abilities. By concentrating on developing our virtues, we can establish the habits and characteristics that will enable us to improve our abilities and performance over time.

Aristotle believed that virtues were not inborn traits or talents but rather character traits that can be refined through practice and effort. For instance, he viewed courage as a virtue that could be developed by practicing brave acts and taking risks. He also believed that wisdom could be learned through reflection and experience.

By focusing on virtue and character, Aristotle suggested that we can foster a mindset that allows us to take on new challenges and strive for excellence in our pursuits. He believed that by adopting a mindset of continuous improvement, we can achieve our full potential and experience a sense of fulfilment and purpose.

Similarly, the stoic philosopher Epictetus emphasised the power of our thoughts and perceptions, asserting that by embracing a growth mindset, we can overcome any obstacle life throws our way.

The wisdom of these philosophers underlines the importance of a growth mindset for personal growth and success. When we believe that we can improve and grow, we are more likely to push ourselves out of our comfort zones, take risks, and achieve our goals. So, if you're looking to cultivate a growth mindset, embrace the power of your potential and commit to working hard to achieve your dreams.

"We are what we repeatedly do. Excellence, then, is not an act, but a habit" - Aristotle

In life, we all have dreams and goals we wish to accomplish, whether they are personal or professional. Often, we strive to become better versions of ourselves but can feel discouraged by a perceived lack of "natural talent." It's easy to look at those who seem to have it all and wonder how they achieved success so effortlessly. However, the truth is that even the most talented individuals had to put in hard work and dedication to reach their current position.

Consider Ed Sheeran, a celebrated singer and songwriter, as a prime example. He dreamt of pursuing a music career but wasn't born with a remarkable voice. However, Sheeran soon realised that 'natural talent' is just one piece of the puzzle – hard work, dedication, and a growth mindset are equally important in the pursuit of success.

In the face of our goals, we may often fall into the trap of perfectionism. We all deep down really want to excel in everything we do, but when we don't perceive ourselves as perfect, the fear of failure can hold us back. It's essential to remind ourselves that failure is a stepping stone to success. Each time we experience a setback, we learn and grow – and in doing so, we move closer to our goals.

A growth mindset has the power to transform our lives. It's crucial to recognise that we have the capability to improve ourselves, and with perseverance, practice, and an open mindset, we can achieve greatness. Let's begin embracing our shortcomings and work towards our goals with a growth mindset – just like Ed Sheeran did.

Exploring the experiences and research shared by some incredible individuals highlights that cultivating a growth mindset can positively impact numerous aspects of our lives, including relationships, career success, and overall happiness. Those with a growth mindset are more likely to persevere through challenges, take risks, and welcome all opportunities to grow. They focus on their strengths while acknowledging and addressing their weaknesses. By perceiving failures as learning opportunities, they become more resilient in the face of adversity.

Adopting a growth mindset allows you to become the best version of yourself. Recognising that every experience presents an opportunity for learning and growth is vital to ensure all possibilities for you are endless.

WHAT IS A SCARCITY MINDSET AND HOW IT CAN HOLD US BACK IN OUR LIVES?

Have you ever found yourself trapped in the thought that there's just not enough to go around? Not enough time, resources, or opportunities for success? If so, you might be experiencing a scarcity mindset. This mindset can hinder us from reaching our goals by fixating on what we lack instead of appreciating what we already have.

While we've previously discussed the scarcity mindset concerning our relationship with money, I feel it is important to recognise that this mindset can affect other aspects of our lives and impede the development of a growth mindset. Believing that resources, such as love, happiness, knowledge, and success, are limited can create strong feelings of fearfulness and powerlessness.

A scarcity mindset can make us feel isolated and overwhelmed, constantly struggling to keep up. These thoughts can drain our motivation, creativity, and inspiration, hindering our potential to pursue our dreams and goals. When we're consumed by what we don't have, we risk overlooking the abundance of opportunities right smacked in our face, having to miss out on our personal growth and fulfilment.

Instead of allowing a scarcity mindset to dominate our thoughts, we must shift to a growth mindset. Seeing the world as a place full of possibilities gives us the green light to accept our challenges as opportunities and believe that our personal definition of success is within reach. By cultivating a mindset of abundance, we can have the key to our full potential and lead a fulfilling and purposeful life.

A scarcity mindset also fuels unhealthy competition with others. When we believe that success is limited, we might resort to aggressive, selfish, and defensive behaviour, straining our relationships in the process. Imagine you're in a long-term romantic relationship with someone you love deeply. Suddenly, your partner starts acting competitive, trying to outdo you in every aspect of your life. What if their behaviour is rooted in a scarcity mindset? This mindset is driven by the fear that resources are scarce, and in this case, your partner may feel that love and affection are limited also. Instead of wanting to work as a team, they start competing for your love and attention.

The danger of a scarcity mindset lies in its ability to create a downward spiral of fear, anxiety, stress, poor decision-making. In terms of the relationship scenario, competition can lead to a breakdown in communication, trust, and intimacy. However, when both partners demonstrate love, support, and open communication, emphasising that there is more than enough to thrive within the partnership, a growth mindset thrives.

When one partner in a romantic relationship earns significantly more money than the other, it's easy to fall into the trap of a scarcity mindset. The partner earning less may feel insecure, jealous, or resentful of their partner's financial success, while the higher-earning partner might define themselves by their financial success and view their partner's lower income as a reflection of their worth.

A scarcity mindset can create friction in this situation and that only leads to feelings of inadequacy and insecurity. The financially successful partner may feel burdened by the responsibility of providing for their partner and question their own value beyond their income. This imbalance of power can breed resentment and strain the relationship.

To combat these negative patterns, a growth mindset encourages both partners to work together to build a life they both desire. When one partner succeeds financially, it should be celebrated as a win for the team, not just for the individual. A growth mindset sees challenges and successes as opportunities to grow stronger as a couple, tackling obstacles as a united front.

Imagine your relationship as a relay race, with both partners working together towards a shared goal: a happy and fulfilling life. When one partner struggles, the other can offer support and guidance, ensuring that both continue moving forward. The same goes for success – when one partner succeeds, both partners should celebrate their collective progress.

Creating this team mentality is crucial in overcoming the pitfalls of a scarcity mindset. Recognising that each partner brings and offers their unique skills and talents to the table allows both of them to appreciate each other's contributions and work collaboratively towards shared goals.

A growth mindset has the power to transform relationships by shifting the focus from individual success to shared achievements. Welcoming those challenges as opportunities to strengthen the partnership creates a sense of unity and support, allowing the relationship to deepen and thrive from that experience.

Ultimately, acknowledging the impact of a scarcity mindset on your relationship is essential in building a strong foundation for long-term success. By adopting an abundance mindset and viewing your partner as an ally, you can create a loving and supportive partnership that leads to a happier, more fulfilling life together. Remember, when you work together, you can accomplish so much more than when you work alone.

So, the next time you find yourself slipping into a scarcity mindset, pause and remind yourself that there's always enough of everything in life. In your relationships and connections, concentrate on shared goals and work collectively to achieve them, regardless of the circumstances. By doing so, you'll discover an abundance of love, happiness, and success, realising that there was never any reason to worry in the first place.

EXPLORING THE BENEFIT OF ADOPTING A GROWTH MINDSET

Listening to Abraham Hicks teachings is one of my favourite pastimes and a scarcity mindset is something that Esther discusses a lot. Abraham teaches us that when we have a scarcity mindset, we tend to focus on the lack of something we desire. This can lead to feelings of frustration, disappointment, and even despair. However, instead of getting caught up in the specifics of what we don't have, we should try to shift our focus to something more general.

Picture this, if you are someone who is struggling financially, instead of fixating on the bills you can't pay or the things you can't buy, focus on the abundance that is already present in your life. You might have fantastic health, be able to breathe full and deep, have a loving circle of people around you like family and friends, or be able to enjoy simple pleasures like a good meal or being able to take a walk outside.

Now, I'm not saying we should ignore our problems or stop trying to reach our goals, but by appreciating what we already have, we can create a solid foundation for growth and happiness. When we start seeing our lives through a lens of abundance, we can shift our energy and become magnets for positivity and opportunity.

When we embrace a growth mindset, we realise that success isn't some finite resource that only a few lucky people get to experience. Nope, success is out there for all of us, and it's up to us to go after it with everything we've got! And you know what's pretty cool? When we see success as an abundant resource, we can genuinely cheer on our friends and family members as they achieve their goals, knowing that their success doesn't take away from ours.

By adopting a growth mindset, we become our own biggest fans, rooting ourselves on through every challenge and setback. We're not afraid to mess up, because we know that those experiences teach us valuable lessons and help us grow. When we believe in ourselves and our potential, the sky's the limit!

So, next time you catch yourself feeling envious or resentful of someone else's achievements, take a step back and remind yourself that there's plenty of success to go around. Remember, we're all on this crazy adventure called life together, and when we lift each other up, we create a world filled with limitless possibilities!

Inspiring Story of a Growth Mindset

So, from everything you've heard, are you ready to supercharge your life with the incredible power of a growth mindset? Trust me, it's an absolute game-changer! This mindset can not only transform your perspective on challenges but also lead to some pretty amazing benefits, like improving your mental health and making you more resilient. In this section, we'll dive into the many advantages of a growth mindset and explore how it can help you become the main character of your life.

Let's take a page out of Viola Davis's book. Her journey to becoming one of the most phenomenal actresses of our time is a prime example of how a growth mindset can help us overcome obstacles and reach our goals.

Despite facing poverty and career setbacks, Davis never threw in the towel. Instead, she looked upon each challenge as a chance to learn and grow, recognising that hard work, dedication, and risk-taking were key ingredients for success.

As Davis once said, "I'm a hard worker. I don't believe in shortcuts. You have to do the work if you want to see the results... I'm always trying to hone my craft, trying to become a better actor." This mindset allowed her to see failure not as a reflection of her talent, but as an opportunity to learn and improve. She transformed her career rejections into creative fuel, morphing her "demoralised state into something that was creative and beautiful."

With a growth mindset, the possibilities for you are endless. Picture a world where every challenge is met with fierce determination, where every setback becomes a stepping stone to success, and where creativity and innovation know no bounds. That world is within your grasp. By accepting the unknown and cultivating a growth mindset, you'll become open-minded, resilient, and fearless in the pursuit of what you truly want.
So, what are you waiting for? Embrace the power of a growth mindset and watch as your life transforms in ways you never imagined. Trust me, you've got this!

Ready to transform into the best version of yourself? Let's explore how a growth mindset can help you unleash your superpowers and tackle stress head-on! This extraordinary mindset doesn't just improve your mental state – it can also work wonders for your physical well-being.

So, the benefits of growth mindset will not only have you conquering challenges and thriving, the evidence is clear: a growth mindset not only fuels personal growth but also enhances your health. A study in the Journal of Personality and Social Psychology found that individuals with a growth mindset engage more in healthy behaviours like exercise and nutritious eating, leading to better cardiovascular health, lower inflammation levels, and even a longer life! So, when you're out there slaying your goals, remember that your growth mindset is also giving your physical health a powerful boost!

But wait, there's more! Imagine having a secret weapon that helps you combat stress and emerge victorious. That's precisely what a growth mindset offers, enabling you to tackle stress with confidence and grace. It's like having your very own stress-busting sidekick, and who doesn't want that?

Now, let's talk about how this connects with the other advantages we've discussed. When we cultivate a growth mindset, we see challenges as opportunities rather than obstacles. This outlook not only empowers us to grow and learn but also helps us view our health as something we can actively improve through dedication and hard work. Just as we invest in learning and personal development, prioritising our health becomes a natural extension of our growth mindset.

In Harv Eker's book, "The Secrets of the Millionaire Mind," he emphasises the importance of cultivating a growth mindset to overcome challenges and create a life that is bigger than our problems. Eker notes that successful people believe, "I create my life," rather than "Life happens to me." They view setbacks as opportunities to grow, reducing stress and increasing resilience, which in turn benefits their overall health and well-being.

In a study published by the American Psychological Association, researchers discovered that a growth mindset can serve as a buffer against stress. Participants with a growth mindset experienced less stress and anxiety compared to those with a fixed mindset, proving that your mindset can truly impact your ability to cope with life's ups and downs.

It's time to get real for a moment. Have you ever felt like your abilities were fixed, never to be improved? I know I have, thinking this is my lot! But the truth is, seizing the opportunity to develop a growth mindset can change all that. It helps you believe in your potential to learn and grow while building your self-esteem and positive outlook. When you view setbacks as learning experiences, you'll build resilience and feel empowered to take on the world. The end result? A more positive self-image, healthy individual and an overall more optimistic view of life. The rewards are priceless!

"Life does not just happen to me, I create my life…"

It's the final leg of our growth mindset benefit adventure and unveil its secret to boosting happiness: Championing others' success! That's right – a growth mindset doesn't just make you more resilient, healthy and accomplished; it also transforms how you view the triumphs of those around you.

Ever found yourself feeling a twinge of envy when someone else achieves something great? We've all been there, but when we're stuck in this cycle of comparison, we only limit our own growth and happiness. A growth mindset flips the script, turning scarcity and competition into abundance and collaboration.

With a growth mindset, you'll cheer others on instead of feeling resentful and adopt growth rather than fearing it. This leads to stronger relationships and bolsters your personal development. As you support others, you'll also create a thriving environment that fuels your success. Being genuinely happy for others knowing that it doesn't dampen anything to do with your success

It's time to embrace the profound wisdom a growth mindset offers: focusing on self-improvement will absolutely open new doors to success and joy filled moments in your life.

Louise's story

Louise, an accomplished entrepreneur with a heart of pure gold, who had already tasted success in her businesses but felt something was holding her back from reaching even greater heights. Despite her profitable ventures, Louise found herself trapped by a scarcity mindset, unable to break through the invisible barrier that separated her from the extraordinary success she wanted.

Recognising that her mindset was limiting her potential, Louise decided that it was time for a change. She took the journey in cultivating a growth mindset, focusing on physical health, resilience, optimism, and openness to new ideas – the very benefits we've explored together. Over time, she transformed challenges into opportunities, and her life began to shift in remarkable ways.

As Louise's growth mindset took root, her discipline, drive, and focus intensified. She started "putting a cap on it" and turned those disbelief in her ability to knowing the capability was there for the taking. This powerful mindset shift enabled her to tap into new business opportunities and elevate her success to new levels.

Gradually, Louise's dedication and hard work paid off. Her company achieved unprecedented growth, her clientele expanded, and she ultimately became the millionaire she always wanted to become. By embracing a growth mindset, Louise not only shattered her previous success ceiling but also positively impacted the lives of those around her massively.

Louise's story reminds us that no matter how successful we may already be, our mindset holds the key to unlocking even greater potential and pushing beyond our perceived limits. If you find yourself longing for more or feeling constrained by self-imposed boundaries, it's time to embrace a growth mindset and witness your world literally expand with opportunities that once seemed hidden from your view. Remember, this transformation takes dedication and effort, but you've seen the rewards and they are nothing short of life-changing. Start cultivating your growth mindset today and elevate your success to extraordinary heights!

PROVIDING A PRACTICAL STRATEGY FOR CULTIVATING A GROWTH MINDSET

You've probably noticed that I'm passionate about championing a growth mindset, and for a good reason! It's the key to unlocking your true potential and achieving your most ambitious goals. Instead of viewing your abilities as fixed, a growth mindset empowers you to see your potential as a dynamic force, capable of evolving through dedication and hard work.

One incredibly effective way to cultivate this mindset is by embracing the power of "yet." When facing challenges or setbacks, it's easy to feel discouraged and doubt your abilities. But by simply adding "yet" to the end of negative thoughts, you can reframe your perspective and open up a world of possibilities.

Picture this: you're training for a marathon, and despite months of effort, you fall short of your distance goal during a recent run. It's natural to feel defeated and think, "I'll never be able to run 26.2 miles." But with a "yet" mindset, you acknowledge your progress and remind yourself that success is still within reach – you just haven't reached your goal... yet.

This powerful mindset shift allows you to view setbacks as opportunities for growth, resilience, and adaptability. It gives you the mental space to reassess, celebrate your progress, and make the necessary adjustments to keep moving forward.

The "yet" mindset is a gateway to endless possibilities for self-improvement and growth. It encourages you to stay motivated, focused, and determined in the face of adversity. By reminding yourself that you are a work in progress, capable of learning and evolving, you'll develop the resilience needed to overcome obstacles and achieve your dreams.

So, how do you start embracing a "yet" mindset? Begin by acknowledging the power of the journey itself, not just the destination. Celebrate the small wins along the way, and remember that every challenge is an opportunity to learn and grow. When faced with a difficult task or slow progress, shift your mindset from defeat to potential by saying, "I don't know how to do this yet, but I'm willing to put in the effort to learn and enjoy the process."

With a "yet" mindset, you'll discover newfound motivation, resilience, and adaptability – all essential ingredients for turning your dreams into reality. So, go ahead and start cultivating a growth mindset today, and watch as your world expands with opportunities that were once hidden from view.

Last but not least, another fantastic way to cultivate a "yet" mindset is to embrace trials and tribulations as your own 'personal growth adventures'. Yeah, it can be tempting to shy away from difficult tasks and stick to what we know. But hey, where's the fun in that? By leaping out of our comfort zones and taking on new challenges, we expand our abilities and unleash the awesome power of personal growth!

Imagine being asked to lead a project at work that's way outside your usual wheelhouse. Instead of letting fear and intimidation take the wheel, see it as your golden ticket to growth-town! Ask yourself, "What can I do to rise to the challenge and totally crush it?" By diving headfirst into new experiences and embracing challenges with open arms, you'll build resilience and rock a growth-oriented mindset that's practically unstoppable.

At the end of the day, nurturing a "yet" mindset is all about refusing to throw in the towel when the going gets tough. It's about turning challenges into opportunities and celebrating every single step forward, no matter how small. So, the next time you're up against a daunting task or what seems like an impossible goal, channel your inner "yet" mindset and prepare to astonish yourself with your own incredible accomplishments. Never forget, you possess the power to reach your goals - progress unfolds one "yet" at a time!

My experience with "yet"

I'll never forget the day I walked back into the gym after months away. As I scanned the room filled with fitness enthusiasts at 4am, my heart plummeted. My fear of injuring my shoulder again gripped me, while everyone else seemed so far ahead in their journeys. I couldn't help but compare myself, feeling deflated and defeated.

But hey, that's when my close ones stepped in and offered a gentle nudge, observing my lack of progress. Instead of drowning in self-pity, I decided it was time for a mindset makeover – enter the mighty "yet" mindset! I realised I might not be crushing my fitness goals at that very moment, but that didn't mean I couldn't; I just wasn't there... yet.

So, I shifted my focus to my own path, cheering on every little victory and embracing my journey's uniqueness. Every gym session, I reminded myself that progress, no matter how small, was still progress! Instead of getting caught up in comparisons, I celebrated others' successes, knowing their achievements didn't diminish mine.

The "yet" mindset wasn't just a game-changer in the gym; it supercharged other areas of my life too! I no longer set limits on what I could accomplish – I dove into new experiences and conquered challenges, leaving self-doubt in the dust.

Now, let's turn the spotlight on you! Reflect on areas of your life where you might be holding yourself back – your career, relationships, or personal growth. Imagine how the "yet" mindset could catapult you into new possibilities! Remember, you might not be where you want to be right now, but with a sprinkle of growth mindset magic, the sky's the limit.

As we wrap up this chapter, remember that it's crucial to nurture a growth mindset in our fast-paced world. It's easy to get trapped in a scarcity mindset, tangled up in self-doubt and fear. But it's time to smash those mental barriers and unleash the go-getter within – see the world as your playground of endless opportunities, abundance, and mind-blowing possibilities!

"The only limits you have are the limits you believe" – Wayne Dyer

Get ready to transform your life because a growth mindset isn't just a mindset – it's a way of life! Embracing challenges, learning from hiccups, and powering through obstacles is what it's all about. When we adopt a growth mindset, we see ourselves as magnificent works in progress, always evolving and improving. This mindset not only boosts our mental health and happiness, but it also leads to epic success and fulfilment in every aspect of life.

Breaking free from a scarcity mindset isn't a walk in the park, but with the right game plan and mindset, it's totally achievable. Throughout this chapter, we've uncovered top-notch strategies for cultivating a growth mindset: rocking the "yet" mindset, reframing negative self-chatter, spotting and conquering limiting beliefs, and learning from disappointments like a champ.

But knowing these strategies isn't enough – we've got to put them into action every single day! Let's make the "yet" mindset our new norm, catch ourselves when we're stuck in negative thinking, and seek out ways to learn from our failures and roadblocks. That's how we'll unleash the life-changing magic of a growth mindset.

So, my friend, it's time to seize the day and put these strategies into practice! You have the power to kick scarcity mindset to the curb and embrace a growth mindset that'll transform your life and inspire those around you. Remember, it's never too late to kickstart your journey of personal growth and self-discovery.

In the wise words of the talented Viola Davis, "The ultimate privilege in life is to become your truest self." So, let's be our authentic selves, adopt that growth mindset, and start living the life we were born to live! The power is in your hands, so act now and experience the limitless possibilities that come with a growth mindset.

Bravo for making it through this chapter on cultivating a growth mindset! You've already taken the first leap towards personal growth, and I'm stoked to be part of your journey.

We've explored the downsides of a scarcity mindset, the awesomeness of a "yet" mindset, and how a growth mindset can boost your mental and physical health. Now it's time to turn knowledge into action.

To get you started, I've cooked up a simple, yet impactful 6-day challenge that'll help you cultivate a growth mindset and reap the rewards in every area of your life. Are you ready to level up? Let's dive in and make it happen!

TASK

Alright, chosen ones, get ready to go on a thrilling 6-day challenge designed to help you unleash your inner growth warrior! Your mission? Identify those fixed mindset moments and actively replace them with an empowering growth mindset. Here's how we'll do it:

Day 1: Mind Over Matter

Kick off the challenge by visualising a challenging task you need to tackle. If any negative self-talk tries to sneak in, don't fret! Consciously choose to reframe those thoughts with a growth mindset twist. So, instead of thinking, "I don't know if I can do this," switch it up to, "I don't know if I can do this **yet**, but hey, I've got the power to learn and adapt!"

Day 2: Embrace Failure

Reflect on a past experience where things didn't go as planned. But here's the catch - instead of dwelling on the negatives, dig for the lessons learned. Write down three golden nuggets of wisdom you gained from the experience and how they can propel you toward future success.

Day 3: Gratitude Journaling

Time to express gratitude for three things that have shaped your personal growth and development. Trust me in saying jot them down, explain their impact, and appreciate the progress you've made so far!

Day 4: Seek Feedback

Reach out to a trustworthy friend or colleague for feedback on a project or task you've recently completed. The challenge? Ditch defensiveness and embrace their constructive criticism as a chance to grow and level up your skills!

Day 5: Celebrate Progress

Take a moment to bask in the glow of your achievements in both your personal and professional life. Note down three accomplishments that make you proud, and let them fuel your motivation to keep pushing forward on your growth journey!

Day 6: Focus on Learning

Choose a fascinating topic you're eager to explore, even if you're a total newbie. Dive into an article, video, or podcast, and let the learning begin! As you take notes and reflect on your new knowledge, remember that learning is an epic journey - every nugget of wisdom brings you closer to mastery.

Cultivating a growth mindset is a lifelong adventure, and this 6-day challenge is just the beginning. Sure, there'll be ups and downs, but by choosing growth, you're taking control of your destiny and creating a brighter future. Remember, progress takes time, but with consistent practice, there's no limit to what you can achieve with your mighty growth mindset! So, let's get this growth party started!

....

....

....

....

....

....

....

....

....

....

....

....

Chapter 12

CONTINUING THE JOURNEY

Well, chosen ones, congratulations on reaching this exciting milestone on your self-development adventure! You've shown incredible courage, resilience, and dedication throughout this journey, and I'm beyond proud of how far you've come. Just remember - this isn't the end; it's only the beginning!

Your quest for personal growth, discovery, and improvement is a lifelong pursuit that demands constant commitment, passion, and awareness. As you continue to grow and evolve, always keep in mind that you're the chosen one - the one who holds the power to shape your destiny, overcome challenges, and unleash your true potential. You're the one who can create an extraordinary life filled with joy, abundance, and purpose. Just stay dedicated to the path of self-discovery, growth, and transformation.

Never forget that you are worthy of love, success, and happiness. No matter what difficulties you face, remember that you're strong and capable of overcoming them. Draw upon the courage, resilience, and inner strength you've cultivated on this journey, and use those qualities to tackle any obstacles that come your way.

Spend some time reflecting on the valuable lessons you've learned and the person you've become. Think about your values, passions, and life's purpose. Consider how you can use your talents, skills, and strengths to create a meaningful and satisfying life. Set new goals, refine your priorities, and map out your future using any insights and wisdom you've gained.

As you continue on your self-development journey, remember that the path won't always be smooth and predictable. There will be highs and lows, twists and turns, and even a few unexpected detours. At times, you'll make significant progress, while at other moments, you may feel stuck or uncertain. But no matter what happens, keep moving forward with optimism, gratitude, and faith in your ability to succeed.

Throughout our time together, we've covered a variety of topics, including self-awareness, resilience, setting and achieving goals, nurturing positive relationships, managing stress, practicing self-care, and pursuing passions. All these elements are important aspects of your self-development journey, but there's one crucial factor that connects them all - **your mindset**.

As you continue on your incredible journey, here are some valuable reminders to keep in mind:

- Celebrate your uniqueness: You're a one-of-a-kind, fantastic individual. Cherish your distinct qualities and never let anyone dampen your spirit.

- Trust in yourself: You possess the strength and potential to achieve anything you set your heart on. Believe in your capabilities and follow your instincts.

- Take action: Dreams are just dreams unless you act on them. Transform your aspirations into reality by taking the necessary steps, no matter how big they may seem.

- Learn from setbacks: Remember, setbacks aren't failures; they're opportunities to grow, learn, and improve. Embrace them as essential parts of your journey towards success.

- Surround yourself with positivity: Be around people who uplift, encourage, and support you in achieving your goals.

- Practice gratitude: Make gratitude a daily habit to shift your mindset and attract more positivity into your life. Reflect on the things you're thankful for each day.

Lastly, I want to express my deepest gratitude for joining me on this self-development adventure. Your courage, dedication, and spirit have been truly inspiring, and I'm certain that the knowledge and growth you've gained will inspire others as well. You are the chosen one, here for a purpose, with a unique destiny to fulfil. You possess all the necessary tools to create the life you desire.

Know that I'm proud of the steps you've taken towards a brighter, more fulfilling future. Never let anyone, including yourself, hold you back from your dreams. Continue growing, learning, and shining your light. The world needs your unique brilliance, and it's been my absolute privilege to be part of your journey.

"The Hardest Thing in This World Is to Live in It... Be Brave. Live. For Me..." – Buffy Summers

Acknowledgements

This book is not just the result of my efforts alone, but a culmination of the love, encouragement, and support I have received from two incredible people in my life.

I would like to thank my mother, whose constant presence, unwavering love, and infinite wisdom have been the foundation of my life.

Mum, your strength, persistence, ambition, and loving kindness have shown me what it means to be a truly remarkable human being and find ways to improve every day. You have been a true guiding light, and your encouragement and words of wisdom have been an emblem of optimism throughout my journey. Without you, none of this would have been possible. Thank you for being my inspiration and my role model.

I would like to express my deepest gratitude to Dave, a true chosen one, and my best friend in the whole world. Dave, you have been there for me through thick and thin, supporting me even when I didn't believe in myself.

Your faith in me, even at my lowest moments, has been instrumental in shaping who I am today. Your constant challenges and unwavering belief in my abilities have pushed me to be the best version of myself. This book, and everything I have achieved, is a testament to your incredible alliance. I am blessed to have you in my life.

This book is for the world but in dedication and acknowledgement of you both.

Love,

MJ

Printed in Great Britain
by Amazon